T0372924

PRAISE FOR *THINK TALK CREATE*

"*Think Talk Create* is a clarion yet compassionate critique of the ongoing dehumanization of work and workplaces, driven by prioritizing quantity over quality, metrics over ethics, and algorithms *über alles*. Replete with illuminating case studies, this mind-opening book shows how to solve thorny business problems by engaging a company's most valuable assets: its employees and consumers. Every leader should read *Think Talk Create* and distribute copies to their team."
—Lou Marinoff, PhD, author of *Plato Not Prozac!*

"*Think Talk Create* is the marvelous process for reconnecting after the isolation we've experienced during the COVID-19 era, enabling us to reach out for the productive engagement and innovation we so sorely need as individuals, in our organizations, and in society. Its roots are ancient, but it is so up-to-the-moment through David Brendel and Ryan Stelzer's pragmatic advice, cogent social commentary, fascinating science, and wonderful storytelling."
—Sandra Sucher, Harvard Business School, coauthor of *The Power of Trust*

"This is one of the very few business books you'll come across that's both deep, practical, and inspired in a way that will spark new ideas for thinking and acting well. There's a revolution growing where business, healthcare, politics, and the other professions are being understood as essentially humane endeavors meant to celebrate and deploy the best of our talents creatively into the world. This wonderful book will help lead the way toward applying such a powerful perspective in whatever you do with others. Highly recommended!"
—Tom Morris, author of *If Aristotle Ran General Motors*

"Brendel and Stelzer counter the dehumanization flourishing unchecked and entrenched in today's workplace. Their applied method of active inquiry—think, talk, create—actually works at fostering high-performing individuals, teams, and organizations. It's the right approach right now."

—Paul Zak, Claremont Graduate University,
and author of *The Moral Molecule*

"Peter Drucker famously said, 'culture eats strategy for breakfast.' Stelzer and Brendel update and elaborate on that concept, with brilliant examples that make this book both enlightening and a roadmap to a more fulfilling workplace and a better future."

—Fred P. Hochberg, former chairman and president,
Export-Import Bank of the United States,
and author of *Trade Is Not a Four-Letter Word*

think
talk
create

Building Workplaces
Fit for Humans

David Brendel and Ryan Stelzer

PUBLICAFFAIRS

New York

PublicAffairs
Hachette Book Group
1290 Avenue of the Americas, New York, NY 10104
www.publicaffairsbooks.com
@Public_Affairs

Printed in the United States of America

First Edition: September 2021

Published by PublicAffairs, an imprint of Perseus Books, LLC, a subsidiary of Hachette Book Group, Inc. The PublicAffairs name and logo is a trademark of the Hachette Book Group.

The Hachette Speakers Bureau provides a wide range of authors for speaking events. To find out more, go to www.hachettespeakersbureau.com or call (866) 376-6591.

The publisher is not responsible for websites (or their content) that are not owned by the publisher.

Library of Congress Cataloging-in-Publication Data
Names: Brendel, David H., author. | Stelzer, Ryan, author.
Title: Think talk create : building workplaces fit for humans / David Brendel and Ryan Stelzer.
Description: New York : PublicAffairs, [2021] | Includes bibliographical references and index.
Identifiers: LCCN 2020055391 | ISBN 9781541730564 (hardcover) | ISBN 9781541730540 (ebook)
Subjects: LCSH: Corporate culture. | Work environment. | Human comfort.
Classification: LCC HD58.7 .B738 2021 | DDC 658.3/12—dc23
LC record available at https://lccn.loc.gov/2020055391

ISBNs: 978-1-5417-3056-4 (hardcover); 978-1-5417-3054-0 (e-book)

LSC-C

Printing 1, 2021

In memory of my father,
Robert J. Brendel

* * *

To Auntie Mary,
and to Git

Contents

That Socrates always smilingly welcomed the contradictions opposed to his reasoning was due, it might be said, to his strength.

—Michel de Montaigne,
On the Art of Conversation

INTRODUCTION

Counting Your Chickens Won't Make Them Hatch

In the 1990s, a professor of animal sciences, William M. Muir, wanted to breed the ultimate egg-laying chicken. He took a large population of hens, housed them nine to a coop, counted the number of eggs produced by each animal, and then selected the top producer from each coop and put her into the breeding pool to create the next generation. To his surprise—after several generations of choosing and breeding only the most productive egg layer from each clutch of nine—what Muir developed was a new strain of hyperaggressive birds. The hens viciously pecked away at each other, leaving them all de-feathered and many of them dead. Egg production plummeted.

More to the point—and in keeping with themes of this book—the professor conducted a parallel experiment to assess group, rather than individual, productivity. He compared the numbers of eggs produced across multiple coops, then put all of the hens—not just the superstars—from the top-performing coop into the breeding pool. After a few generations, each of the hens was alive, healthy, and fully feathered. Egg productivity soared 160 percent.[1]

Getting chickens to lay more eggs can take us only so far as a guide to how humans ought to behave when they're working together, but we found this story instructive for two reasons. First, we liked the note of caution about selecting only one individual—especially on the basis of a single quantitative metric. With chickens, this didn't work because often the best egg producer was simply the most ferocious bird, the one who most aggressively pecked at her coop mates, sometimes to the point of killing them. Second, the story reminds us that even in such an individualized activity as pushing eggs out your rear end, success depends heavily on your social environment. In other words, coops filled with nothing but scratching, clawing, and measuring are not optimal environments for getting things done, much less done creatively.

In this book, we examine the retrograde "scratch and claw" mindset that has overtaken the world of work: the ruthless pursuit of numbers and productivity above all else. But we also provide a clear idea for replacing this mindset with something better. The only thing capable of deconstructing the inhumanity present in today's professional world is humanity. And what uniquely defines us as human beings? Our ability to think, talk, and create. The Think Talk Create model we offer here is a disciplined methodology for making professional and organizational environments more enjoyable and inspiring, as well as more innovative and successful. In addition, we'll show that by applying this new methodology not only will companies and organizations be better positioned for success, but all stakeholders—employees, customers, patients, and innocent bystanders—will benefit as well.

The primary problem among so many organizations today is that they've taken the perfectly reasonable management adage that "what gets measured gets done" and pushed it to such an extreme that the numbers are all that matter. As a result—and as was the case with Muir's chickens—the well-being of each individual, as well as the overall performance of the group, suffers. Moreover, this obsession with numbers puts society as a whole at risk.

Modern physics teaches us that light can act as a wave or a particle, depending on the context and how it's measured. Likewise, human activity can be measured in many ways, depending on the perspective we choose to take. In business, we too often think exclusively about the bottom line, neglecting other phenomena—respect, collaboration, trust, social cohesion—that are actually essential determinants of achieving the long-term success we're looking for.

Until very recently, the most egregious example of the quantitative mindset driven into the ground was the shortsighted but all-too-prevalent belief that "the CEO's only responsibility is to increase shareholder value." This obsession with a single metric (return on investment) has meant that, for the past several decades, other stakeholders (the customers, the community, the employees, the environment) have gotten the short end of the stick. Making matters far worse, especially in new and disruptive industries, the "numbers guy" is often hidden inside a machine—literally an algorithm. Similarly, medical-treatment algorithms have resulted in certain advances, but in too many cases have compromised personalized medical care and, in some worst-case scenarios, led to unnecessary death.

Looming over our numbers-obsessed society is another overly revered metric—GDP—that tells us nothing about social progress or quality of life or any other meaningful benchmark. All GDP tells you is how much stuff gets produced. According to this narrow and myopic metric, the value of mastering the violin, or of teaching children to read, or of making sure they have clean air to breathe is nothing compared to the value of producing tons of steel or rubber or what have you. And this value distortion holds true even when the valued commodities are taken to the desert and blown up, which is the kind of thing nations often find themselves doing when they value quantitative goals over human principles.

Extend the mindless pursuit of higher GDP numbers globally and you find yourself staring down the biggest big-picture question of them all, which is whether our species will survive. In 2019, the United Nations released a study authored by its Intergovernmental Science-Policy Platform on Biodiversity and Ecosystem Services, drafted by a host of social and physical science experts, which offered a grim reality check on the future of our planet by the numbers. More than one million species—one-eighth of all of earth's plants, insects, and animals—face extinction in just a matter of decades. The authors of this landmark study concluded without equivocation that the "relentless global pursuit of economic growth is driving the collapse of life on earth."[2]

Separately and together, we've spent our careers at leading institutions, including the White House and Harvard Medical School. Based on our experiences working in these challenging environments, we decided to write a book that intersects with the worlds of academia, health care, business, and government, putting forth a proactive methodology—Think Talk Create—that knows no industry limitations or professional borders. In each of these domains, we've witnessed institutional deterioration and stress-related illness due to an insipid, mind-numbing, and hostile management style focused far too much on the numbers and not nearly enough on the people. As a result, we often find ourselves counseling professionals who are standing on the metaphorical—and sometimes literal—ledge, about to jump. This book emerges directly from our professional odysseys, which have led us to recognize and diagnose the pervasive common cold of our modern-day working world: the overreliance on numerical thinking to the exclusion of all else.

We're hardly the first to push back against the "shareholder value über alles" ideas of people like economist

Milton Friedman and Harvard Business School professor Michael Jensen. And plenty of others—most recently Shoshana Zuboff in *The Age of Surveillance Capitalism*—have sounded the alarm over the encroachment of algorithms and artificial intelligence into every aspect of our lives. The push and pull between quantitative and humanistic mindsets, between what we can know about ourselves reductively and what will always be inexplicable, goes back millennia and remains with us today, informing discussions about economics and health care and every other domain of existence. In a recent *New York Times* article, Amir Alexander, a historian of mathematics, described this conflict as "a long struggle pitting the human advocates of mathematics and order against an unruly world that seems to keep its deepest mysteries to itself."[3]

Math and empirical science have gained the upper hand, and there's no doubt that they've made a huge contribution to our well-being. But, as we shall see, human complexities always intrude, and we disregard those subtle and disruptive forces—emotion, meaning, purpose, individualism—at our peril.

French biologist Jean Rostand said that "science has made us gods even before we are worthy of being human."[4] We're still struggling to figure out how to incorporate an explosion of data and technology into our everyday lives. This is especially true in corporate and professional settings, where we continually grapple with such necessities as financial metrics, computer algorithms, evidence-based medicine, and other quantitative resources that are helpful but, if left unchecked, can take on a destructive life of their own. How do we make sure the tail doesn't wag the dog? How, in other words, can we guarantee that these technologies don't determine the course of human lives but are, instead, leveraged in the service of our common values? We can't just be tech gods. We will be worthy of being human only when we figure out why we've developed such sophisticated math and science in the first place and understand to what purposes we should apply them.

Where this book is radically different is not just in offering a critique but in trying to move the discussion forward by presenting an alternative mental construct, a fundamentally different, comprehensive way of viewing human work interactions that requires us to step back before we can step forward.

Our approach to improving both the lives of individuals and the performance of organizations is based on AI—but not the kind critics of technology gone awry worry about. Our "AI" doesn't involve anything silicon based. Instead, it refers to a very human process known as active inquiry, the polar opposite of the top-down, command-and-control, strictly by-the-numbers approaches that have prevailed for decades (even when the decision-making is supposedly distributed, or evolving through machine learning).

Active inquiry is as ancient as the Acropolis and as current as the latest research in neurobiology. It melds old and new to examine the influences that allow human beings to succeed—which includes being highly productive at work. Think Talk Create is the practicum for active inquiry; it's the disciplined, step-by-step process that allows active inquiry to take hold and drive results.

Tens of thousands of years ago—probably the first time a tribe of humans had enough to eat and a few hours with no immediate mortal threat—people began to think about what it all means, which gave rise not just to religion but to what would flower among the Greeks as philosophy. We both pursued graduate degrees in philosophy, buttressing our professional skills with humanistic concepts such as value, truth, and meaning. It was these ideas that influenced our thinking about how individuals, companies, and communities can thrive.

Active inquiry, derived from our time studying the ancient Greeks, teaches individuals how to think carefully about a challenge or opportunity, how to engage peers in dialogue via open-ended questioning, and how to collaboratively build a strategy. Through this process, our kind of AI—active inquiry—cultivates respect and empathy, establishes trust, defines collective values, and, as a result, increases innovation and ultimately financial performance. The so-called soft skills, it turns out, constitute a hard science.

But active inquiry is no quick fix. Nor is it the idea of the month to be discussed at this year's corporate retreat, only to be replaced by next year's model. In keeping with that old adage about teaching someone to fish and they have food for life, active inquiry teaches you how to live your life in an entirely new way—which is also a very old way.

Socrates, an inspirational figure for us, attempted to solve the difficult problems of his society, but as far as we know he never picked up a stylus to make a single calculation. Instead, he spent his days having in-depth conversations with his fellow citizens of Athens. He'd gather a group, ask open-ended questions—questions that do not have simple yes-or-no answers—and together they would try to reach some kind of insight and truth. It was a remarkably effective technique—in philosophy it's still taught as the "Socratic method"—because it empowered partners in conversation to engage in both self-discovery and collaborative reasoning.

Active inquiry represents our best opportunity to engage each other in meaningful collaboration, but to succeed it requires self-reflection and self-restraint. While appearing deceptively simple on the surface, active inquiry depends on careful construction of questions that don't contain even subtle judgments or biases. It must be truly open-minded and focused on learning, free of preconceived notions. The commitment to listening and learning must be paramount. We must aspire to be excellent conversation partners, applying as much seriousness and focus as we do in our analytical work in science, technology, medicine, and business in a data-driven world.

As a result, active inquiry, and the process of Think Talk Create, can be developed and honed only with intensive practice. On the surface, the methodology appears so obvious and straightforward that many people hardly pay it any mind. But it turns out to be the most difficult and elusive skill necessary in the modern quantitative era. The time and effort to learn it are well worthwhile, with impressive pay-offs for quality of life, human dignity, and profitability in a capitalist society. We demonstrate throughout this book how the process can play out through the lens of real-world narratives.

What both artificial intelligence and active inquiry have in common is a facility for learning. But neither the AI machine nor the inquiring human brain is fully hardwired, whether by software code or genetic code. Instead, both are plastic—that is, highly adaptive to new challenges. They engage in self-organization, responding not in a fixed, pre-programmed manner to inputs but instead in a bottom-up, agile fashion. In active inquiry, dialogue is the primary driver of learning and self-organization. The applicable "machine" is inside our skulls, and it consists of networks of about eighty-six billion nerve cells, with unfathomable interconnectedness. Numbers are important inputs, but to avoid catastrophically bad decisions, conversation, nuanced judgment, and complex decision-making are also required.

People working in teams to get things done care about results—as do the people they report to—so can the soft skills we're talking about deliver the goods? How do active inquiry and attentiveness to humanistic values stack up against hiring the best people with the best technical chops?

In 2012, that most quantitative of companies, Google, embarked on Project Aristotle, a two-year study to discover what makes the perfect team. The researchers found that individual expertise was not the secret sauce. In fact, in a finding that harkens back to William Muir and his chickens, no characteristic of any individual team member or members explained the success of the best-performing groups. Instead, it was an emergent property of the team as a whole, psychological safety, that turned out to be most essential. And what does psychological safety mean? It is an interpersonal dynamic in which each individual feels encouraged and empowered to share ideas and insights proactively. In 1990, William Kahn defined psychological safety as "being able to show and employ one's self without fear of negative consequences of self-image, status or career."[5] It's been championed in recent years by Amy Edmondson, a professor at Harvard Business School, whose research has shown that the absence of psychological safety can lead to "colossal business failure."[6]

For further endorsement of the kind of trust building and open dialogue we prescribe, consider, if you will, the following:

- In one study, nearly one hundred managers were broken into small groups and asked to solve a specific strategic challenge. But before they could begin brainstorming, one group was asked to go around and share personal stories of success, while the other group was asked to share personally embarrassing stories. After just ten minutes of conversation, the teams that had shared embarrassing stories generated 26 percent more ideas than those that had shared personal success stories. A psychologically safe environment—in this case, an environment in which people had been willing to reveal their foibles and vulnerability—fosters creativity and enhances performance. It allows ideas to be shared freely and teams to collaborate without fear of judgment, reprisal, or loss of status.[7]

- The *Wall Street Journal* has found that employees who underwent empathy training generated up to 50 percent more net income than those who did not participate.[8]

- When the University of Southern California crisscrossed the globe asking business leaders what attributes executives must have to succeed in today's digital, globalized economy, they identified five essential characteristics: adaptability, cultural competence, intellectual curiosity, empathy, and 360-degree thinking.[9] Each of these core characteristics can be enhanced through our version of AI, active inquiry.

- The Carnegie Institute of Technology at Carnegie Mellon University has found that approximately 85 percent of financial success is related to skills in "human engineering" (personality and ability to communicate, negotiate, and lead) while only 15 percent is related to technical proficiency.[10] Similarly, a comprehensive 2006 study led by Accenture found that interpersonal competence, self-awareness, and social awareness were better predictors of success than conventional quantitative metrics.[11]

- Kara Swisher, a *New York Times* contributing opinion writer about technology, has reported that the latest trend among high-flying tech companies is hiring a CEO. No, not the extravagantly compensated executive in the corner office with no paper on their desk. In this instance, after so many episodes of inappropriate sharing of customer data and inadvertent collusion with foreign despots, the new, in-demand CEO is the chief ethics officer. It seems that brilliant mathematical minds designing near-magical technology can get into serious hot water without the help of a good old-fashioned moral compass.[12]

- Research from Stanford and the World Economic Forum has shown that work is one of, if not the greatest, source of anxiety, depression, and stress-related disorders.[13] Suicide rates have skyrocketed 24 percent during the past fifteen years, and a 2015 study published in the *American Journal of Preventive Medicine* concluded that one of the primary factors for this spike was "distress about jobs."[14] The primary demographic affected by suicidal ideation is adults of working age, and it's been shown to plague groups ranging from call-center workers to hedge-fund managers, accountants, doctors, lawyers, consultants, and all in between.

- Finally, an endorsement from the unlikeliest of places: management consulting, where a large-scale consulting operation showed equanimity, respect, and an eye to long-term growth and profitability in its response to the global COVID-19 pandemic— something that was seemingly impossible for a number of dysfunctional governments in their poorly orchestrated responses. Using active inquiry to its advantage, this company sought to improve its organizational culture in the midst of COVID-19 chaos instead of telling employees to suck it up because times are hard for everybody.

Quantitative metrics leave little room for the supposedly soft human realities such as the need for empathy, connection, and meaning. The "quant jocks" have actually put us back with the hunter-gatherers—before they found that first moment by the fire to scratch some animal pictures and wonder about the meaning of existence. The quantitative marching orders are, "The only reason you need for doing this is so you can keep on doing it. Raw survival. A full belly. Nobody says you're supposed to like it. Nobody says you're supposed to care. Just make your numbers." This is as true for a hedge-fund manager as it is for an Amazon warehouse worker. The "master of the universe" may have more creature comforts and amazing vacations, but workers all across the income spectrum share the same stark reality: whatever you've got, make your numbers or it all goes away. In the words of Tennyson: "Nature, red in tooth and claw."

Yet the latest science shows us that the human brain evolved to its current size and complexity largely because greater size and complexity provided two advantages for survival that had very little to do with individual aggression and competition. These are the ability to manage relationships within a larger and more complex social group and the ability to piece together random and chaotic experience into a consistent narrative—that is, to make meaning, which is the only way you can begin to think about making tomorrow better than today. So when critics say that what we're offering sounds "soft," and that they want approaches that are hard-headed and "scientific," we invite them to update their knowledge of science.

Another old adage says that crisis brings opportunity. For all the pain and dislocation the COVID-19 pandemic has caused—at least by rattling everyone's routine, if not their sense of personal safety—it has rekindled questions of value and meaning for millions of people. Socially isolated and forced to think about death as an all-too-real daily possibility, many of us have reflected on modern organizations' imposition of a Hobbesian view of life as "nasty, brutish, and short." Many of us chimed in with Peggy Lee, singing, "Is that all there is?" We've also opened our eyes to just how bankrupt and foolish this "don't ask questions, just march" view is, especially when it flies in the face of what we've learned from modern neuroscience, evolutionary biology, and behavioral economics.

"What, after all, is the economy's purpose?" Paul Krugman asked in a *New York Times* op-ed in response to the pandemic. "If your answer is something like, 'To generate incomes that let people buy things,' you're getting it wrong—money isn't the ultimate goal; it's just a means to an end, namely, improving the quality of life." And what's the best way to begin to enhance quality of life? "Not dying," he concludes.[15] And yet some employers have pushed their workers to maintain productivity during the COVID-19 crisis without providing adequate protections to prevent disease transmission—the ultimate dehumanizing workplace.

This book takes the opposite approach. It draws on the work of cutting-edge researchers such as Paul Zak, the founder of neuroeconomics, who showed us the power of trust in economic development, and Daniel Kahneman, who showed us how misguided it is to appeal only to human rationality, especially what mid-twentieth-century economics called "rational self-interest." A new wave of science has shown that linear rationality is simply not the way the human mind and human motivation operate. We are highly irrational creatures, deeply emotional and deeply social, and our sense of social and emotional well-being has a huge influence on how well we perform. A complex, often surprising human being lurks behind the numbers, undermining our evidence-based predictions of how they'll behave. We are living in a post-Newtonian world, where theory and research in quantum physics have revealed how indeterminate and uncertain existence really is. If that sounds soft, we say, "Welcome to the future."

In organizing and codifying a force to oppose dehumanization, we offer Think Talk Create as a rigorous approach to collaborative learning and problem-solving. In medicine, it's important to give the patient relief from immediate symptoms, but it's also necessary to address the underlying disease. Similarly, an organization that's under the gun can make any number of financial and operational adjustments to produce a healthier-looking quarterly report, but that's just symptomatic relief. We need to go more toward the root of the matter, and active inquiry paves the way. It exhorts us to keep an open mind, gain essential information, and diagnose tricky human problems hidden under reams of quantitative data. It also helps us to treat work-related challenges by fostering transformational conversations and constructing novel solutions. All of this empowers a more energized work environment, a more successful organization, and the safer, healthier community needed to sustain it over the long haul.

The book unfolds as follows: We'll delineate in Chapter 1 the Think Talk Create methodology, showing through a couple of narratives exactly how it can be used to solve thorny workplace problems and restore the better angels of our nature. But what basic workplace conditions are required for Think Talk Create? We'll explore the fundamental importance of psychological safety in Chapter 2 by describing its research base and sharing a vignette that reveals its power. Then, in Chapter 3, we'll show how active inquiry, when performed in psychologically safe contexts, is a critical data-gathering tool. Two narratives (from the worlds of psychiatry and neurology) reveal how we ought to be as rigorous with active inquiry as we are in applying more conventional evidence-based medicine, lest we compromise the quality of care for vulnerable patients.

Scientific experts in medicine and other fields are at serious risk of developing trained incapacity, through which they are blinded to relevant interpersonal cues because they're hyper-focused on what they know in the most depth. In Chapter 4, we'll present the story of the cofounder of a tech company whose trained incapacity, combined with his disregard for the emotional states of others when he stepped into the office, became his undoing—and how his later training (via executive coaching) in active inquiry skills led him to make satisfying career progress and improve his family life.

Along the way, in Chapter 4 and elsewhere, we describe some of the neurobiology that can either doom us to fear-based workplaces or elevate us to build work environments that are better suited to human flourishing. The amygdala, seated deep in the brain's limbic system, is the primary driver of fight or flight. If its firings aren't well modulated by the more strategic executive brain, housed in the frontal lobe, then really bad things can happen. Individuals fear and mistreat each other; groups deteriorate as a result of hostility, bullying, and distrust. This all occurs against the backdrop of a maniacal focus on productivity, profitability, and un-bridled growth. It's a perfect storm, resulting in a torrent of dehumanization.

The dehumanized workplace is the abiding concern of this book and the prime reason we've developed the Think Talk Create model as a remedy. Chapters 4, 5, and 6 present the health and economic risks of workplaces that are ill-fitted for humans. We come at the problem from a variety of per-spectives, drawing on social-science research and vignettes about individuals who've suffered (or even lost their lives) on the job. We provide historical context, tracing progress from the days of sweatshops, when workers had no rights and a quality of life not much above slavery; to the mid-twentieth-century rise of a thriving middle class; to the reversals driven by shareholder-value-only thinking that have led to huge perks and prosperity for those in the top 1 or 2 percent, eco-nomic stagnation and the gig economy for those below, and debilitating stress and alienation all around.

There is, nonetheless, good reason for hope if we seek it and cultivate it. When the Think Talk Create process is deployed well over time, we can see impressive stakeholder engagement, community development, and financial gain. The upbeat saga of a professional sports team, presented in Chapter 7, reveals how respectful listening to impassioned fans can yield long-term rewards. We see here how active inquiry can help to leverage the findings of behavioral eco-nomics, which has taught us that people (sports fans or otherwise) make important spending decisions primarily on the basis of emotional driving forces rather than rational self-interest. The economic vitality that flows from this dynamic can be a source of delight for all involved.

In the final chapters, we explore the "will to believe," William James's notion, backed up by cognitive psychology research, that we can (and must) choose what we think and how to live. Each of us—regardless of our status at work or station in life—can make meaningful choices with outsize influence. The narratives we share in this book include people from all walks of life. They are custodians, Walmart workers, doctors, young entrepreneurs, a bookstore clerk, an insurance adjuster, a public health advocate, and a tech company cofounder. Their diversity of background and position reveals our common humanity. You don't have to be the CEO to make a profound difference. We all have agency. We present Think Talk Create for anyone—regardless of what you do—who's interested in building a better world, together.

1

THE HUMAN VARIABLE

Putting People into the Equation

A ten-year-old boy was maimed in a car accident some years ago. He not only suffered multiple physical injuries and was paralyzed from the waist down, but he experienced severe post-traumatic emotional stress. It was obvious that he'd require long-term care. The question was whether the insurance company of the driver at fault would consider only its quarterly balance sheet, or its social and moral responsibility as well, in deciding how to deal with the claim. It was indisputable that the driver of the other automobile had been primarily at fault, having broadsided the car in which the ten-year-old was riding. The boy's father was likely speeding on the highway at the time of the accident, but the police report was clear that the other driver was mostly responsible for the accident. The boy's father carried a $45,000 insurance policy and the insurer paid that amount to the boy in full. The other driver carried a much more generous $500,000 policy. How much of that amount was the boy going to receive?

As in most cases of this sort, the file was given to a claims adjuster, in this instance a man named Jay, a longtime employee of the insurance company. Jay had seen thousands of sad and devastating cases of this kind, and his job was to avoid unnecessary litigation by negotiating an insurance payout to the opposing party. Not to put too fine a point on it, but his job as a claims adjuster was to help his company save money by minimizing the amount paid to the aggrieved individual bringing the claim; to manage, in other words, the bottom line. The negotiation usually involved a back-and-forth with the claimant (or the claimant's attorney), which resulted in a payment to the victim of the accident. During his career, Jay had used his skills to save his company millions of dollars every year. He was a friendly but firm negotiator who knew how to get to yes, quickly close the file, and move on.

But even to this seasoned veteran, the case of a maimed and paralyzed child felt different. This was not a situation in which hard-nosed negotiation felt appropriate. Jay's job had forced him to take some tough positions over the years, but here it felt like playing hardball would be unsavory, if not downright immoral.

On the face of it, the boy's permanent injuries and need for prolonged medical care made it a no-brainer to offer the boy's attorney most (or perhaps all) of the $500,000 that the policy allowed. Jay had three young sons not too far in age from the ten-year-old victim. How much money did Jay think his sons would deserve if, God forbid, they'd been in such an accident? Jay felt that he could convince his boss that this was not the time to protect their margins by making the opposing attorney fight for every cent.

It was all the more shocking, then, when Jay received a call from the boy's attorney, who opened with, "Do you think you could quickly get me $250,000 for the case and we'll be done with it?" This was a young, inexperienced lawyer from a rural village in upstate New York. Had the low cost of living in his area warped his judgment as to what his ten-year-old client would need in the years to come? Was this young lawyer in a rush for some personal reason, not thinking beyond his own eagerness to pocket his share of the settlement?

Sitting in his Manhattan office, Jay knew he could have a quick win here and look like a hero for saving his company a quarter of a million dollars. But he couldn't get beyond the plight of the young boy and his beleaguered parents. A payout of $250,000 from Jay's company, even with the $45,000 they'd already received from their own insurance company, would never be enough to cover the boy's long-term needs.

Jay was facing the core dilemma of the numbers-first culture of our times. Should executives make their decisions on the basis of profitability alone? Is shareholder value the only issue here? Or should other principles—such as social responsibility and corporate reputation—come into play in a meaningful fashion? The reality facing Jay, if he played by the book, indicated a clear course of action. But the human factors lurking behind those numbers suggested a path aligned with the Think Talk Create model. Jay was going to need to step back, navigate his thoughts clearly, engage in some meaningful conversations, and orchestrate a solution that would allow him to sleep at night. Think Talk Create gave Jay the framework to not only do the right thing, but also strategically resolve a complex challenge.

Intuitively, Jay followed those steps as he navigated this financial and ethical dilemma. It wouldn't make sense, he reasoned, to call the boy's attorney back too quickly. Jay wasn't even sure what he'd say at that point. The basic well-being of a child was at stake, and a strict focus on efficiency and the company's balance sheet was surely going to fall short. He needed to consider all the angles, which meant that the first thing to do was slow down and think.

The Methodology

Think Talk Create is a continuous three-step process that always loops back upon itself. Each of the components are dynamically interdependent, the polar opposite of one-and-done thinking. A high-performing work environment doesn't become that way because somebody engaged in active inquiry just once. Instead, high-performing environments are the result of individuals and teams repeatedly using Think Talk Create to their advantage, applying the methodology across multiple circumstances and scenarios when solving a complex problem. We need to think and talk and create, then loop back to thinking some more and talking some more and fine-tuning our creative developments. We can use the process as a whole to tackle step one of the puzzle, then redeploy it when addressing step two of the very same puzzle, and so on.

But when we face a new challenge, as Jay did when the injured boy's file landed on his desk, it's critical to start out with the Think step. The methodology can't get off the ground if we don't slow ourselves down in the midst of our overly busy lives and frenetic workdays. We must pause and remind ourselves that we don't know everything of relevance just yet—and we should think vigorously about alternative perspectives. This calm, flexible, self-reflective mindset lays the foundation for Think Talk Create; it is the basis for avoiding impulsive, short-sighted decision-making. It might start with a few deep, mindful breaths, or taking a walk outside to clear your head, or really finding any old way you like to disconnect temporarily from the familiar surges of stress we all can experience during the workday.

Slowing down and thinking is the essential precondition for the second step of the methodology: Talk. This is where nonjudgmental, open-ended questions come into play. A true open-ended question is well sculpted and mustn't be a conversation stopper. Closed-ended questions, which call forth simple yes-or-no answers, tend to shut down exploratory exchanges and impede learning. Open-ended questions instead elicit free-flowing responses and mutual learning. Fostering conversations rooted in open-ended questions—active inquiry—can provide jet fuel for brainstorming and innovation. We will delineate how Jay did it and later take an even closer look at what active inquiry is all about and how to do it.

We must approach the Talk phase with a truly open mind, a tabula rasa upon which we might sketch out an unforeseen and productive, even inspiring, narrative. The process requires self-restraint and self-discipline. In fact, we might think of the process as a relational form of evidence-based science. Statisticians carefully structure their work around the null hypothesis, which, at the outset of a research study, presumes no difference between interventions (as in the treatment outcome from a placebo versus an active drug). The realm of law provides another angle on this learning-oriented mindset. Just think of the statue of Lady Justice, blindfolded and steadily gripping a beam balance that is not yet tipping one way or the other.

The Talk step requires that, like an empirical scientist or a judge presiding in court, we embark upon our work as free of biases and predetermined ideas as humanly possible. Like Jay, we start out with some basic principles—respect for others, fidelity to a job role—but at the same time remain blank slates about how best to apply those principles collaboratively.

Once we have slowed down to think and talk open-mindedly with those around us, we can enter the third phase, Create, in which we bring something new and meaningful into play: a novel solution to a pesky problem. It might be a new product, service, marketing strategy, or even a whole new organization that can move the world in surprising, positive directions. In Jay's case, it was a well-crafted agreement and plan to ensure that the unfortunate young boy and his family would have appropriate financial resources well into the future. Jay's use of the Think Talk Create process empowered a virtuous result for the boy while securing a sound financial result for his corporation and also preserving its respectability and reputation.

A Humane Solution

Like so many workers, Jay was usually overwhelmed by the multitude of items on his to-do list. Multitasking is antithetical to sustained, focused attentiveness to a complex matter. But the boy's plight was so moving that Jay was able to strip away the usual chaos of multitasking to focus for the rest of the day and into the evening. He developed a well-constructed question that lent itself to further self-reflection and conversations with others via the process of active inquiry. He used his quiet time that day to carefully frame his dilemma: How can I align my responsibility to my company with my humanity and my compassion for the injured boy?

Having refined all the swirling issues into this explicit formulation, Jay was ready to move on to the next phase of the process: talk with others to gain multiple perspectives, troubleshoot ideas, and test his own feelings. He started at home, with his wife and sons. He gave them all the facts in front of him, then asked a number of open-ended questions: What's the right thing for me to do here? What's my most important responsibility? What would you do if you were me?

In an instance of "out of the mouths of babes," one of his sons shrugged his shoulders and offered a truth so simple that Jay staggered under the weight of it. "I thought insurance companies were supposed to pay people when they get hurt."

There was a beautiful logic in that simple formulation. It gave Jay the confidence he needed to follow through with his instinct that his priority should be seeing that the boy was treated fairly. It also helped that his whole family agreed.

Before going to his boss, and wanting to explore other perspectives, Jay reached out to talk with some of his fellow claims adjusters. Fortunately, no one expressed a ruthless, "your job is to nail 'em to the wall" attitude. Instead, their comments focused on the tension they all maintained, trying to be a good employee and a decent human being. The consensus was that cases like this underscored the importance of having a moral code. All the angles and tortured calculations fall away when you decide to simply do what's right. But that begs the question: In complex matters, how can you know what's right beforehand? As Hemingway said, morality is what feels good after.

Jay was now ready to take the final step, which was to create a reasonable solution for all parties, especially the young boy. He got the attorney on the phone, and he continued to follow the active inquiry process by not racing ahead to a predetermined position. Instead, after exchanging pleasantries, Jay asked, "What's your sense of the boy's long-term care needs?" The open-ended question allowed Jay to obtain even more insight into the boy's situation and the attorney's mindset without yet committing to any particular outcome. This prompted the attorney to say, "Hmm, that's a good question. I haven't really thought that through. I was more focused on getting my client's family the money they need now to pay some immediate medical bills."

But Jay's open-ended question had shifted the terms of the conversation away from short-term exigencies and toward the bigger picture. It prompted the attorney to become more reflective and curious. With trust and honesty building between Jay and the attorney, a remarkable thing happened next. The attorney acknowledged that he hadn't been practicing for too long and this was his biggest case so far. He noted that the one-third payment he would take from a $250,000 settlement would represent more money than he'd ever made on a case (and almost as much as his total earnings the year before). He'd been tempted to settle it quickly and win what seemed like a huge amount of money for both him and his client.

Jay and the attorney came to agree that the boy deserved better. "What would be a fairer dollar amount for your client?" Jay asked. "How about $300,000?" the attorney replied. Jay paused to think some more. The new proposal would get the attorney $100,000 and the boy $200,000. Jay asked, again in a calm and nonjudgmental manner, "How would you feel about earning $100,000 for yourself in this case?" The attorney quickly replied that he'd be thrilled—it was far more than he could have anticipated.

With all of this new information, Jay was now poised to make a strong proposal that he was confident would be accepted and would satisfy the interests of all parties involved. "How about this?" Jay started. "My company will pay $450,000 on this $500,000 policy, as long as you agree that the boy will receive $350,000 and you'll limit your fee to $100,000." Jay realized that a payment of $350,000 to the boy was more than he would have received if the attorney had taken one-third of the total $500,000 policy (in that case, the boy would've only received $333,000).

By walking through a Think Talk Create process, Jay had crafted an innovative solution that truly was best for all concerned. It ensured that (1) the boy received a reasonable amount of insurance money in light of what he'd suffered; (2) the attorney would earn more money than under his own proposed settlement; and (3) Jay's company saved $50,000 off the $500,000 they would've likely paid if the case had gone to court, not to mention their own attorney's fees. The quantitative advantages to all parties were clear. Moreover, Jay had constructed a solution that was consistent with his ethical values—it "felt good after"—and also with the company's stated mission of serving the community and being a responsible corporate citizen.

Long-Term Gains

Because it incorporates multiple perspectives and a focus on the big picture, Think Talk Create naturally tends toward win-win solutions, which generally are the ones that accomplish what they purport to and that stay in place for the long run. Successful negotiations aren't about crushing or obliterating your opponent. Things generally work out much better when all sides come away reasonably satisfied and respecting each other. After all, the people we deal with in this way are our customers, business partners, neighbors, and fellow citizens. They help create the world we live in, and very likely our paths will cross again.

Whether you believe in karmic retribution, a moral code, or simple pragmatism, looking beyond short-term gain and doing the right thing is certainly the better way to go. History is full of examples, among the most notable the contrast between the long-term results following World War I and World War II. In 1919, at the Versailles peace conference, France, which had suffered nearly two million casualties and seen the devastation of much of its territory, sought to exact vengeance on Germany by imposing severe restrictions on rearmament and by demanding the payment of harsh reparations. These conditions destroyed the German economy and fueled the geopolitical grievances that led directly to World War II. In contrast, in the wake of that second war, the United States extended generous financial aid and other forms of assistance to rebuild Japan and Germany, the nations it had just defeated, which helped fuel the remarkable peace and prosperity that existed through most of the developed world during the 1950s and beyond.

The success of this forward-looking approach hinges on disciplined conversation guided most fundamentally by open-ended questions. In international relations, this is usually referred to as diplomacy. In the insurance industry, it might be the negotiating stance of a man like Jay. Wherever in the world we find ourselves, this is hard work indeed. Philosophers have grappled with the challenge for millennia. As we touched upon in the introduction, our inspiration and model for Think Talk Create are the ancient Greeks, primarily Socrates—the master of engaging people in meaningful conversations about broad concepts such as justice, beauty, and truth. His inquiry helped people uncover their assumptions, deepen their insight, and confront complex matters head-on. Jay was a modern-day Socrates who brought to the office a penchant for good questions, inquiry, truth seeking, and virtue.

But no one is perfect, and we all can fall into the trap of presumptuous non-learning and giving inquiry short shrift, especially when we're harried, overwhelmed, or stressed out. Not even our revered mentor was exempt from a pitfall we all must guard against. While Socrates's queries almost always appeared open-ended, he occasionally asked his interlocutor leading questions designed to move the dialogue toward his preestablished conclusion. For example, in the dialogue *Euthyphro*, Socrates speaks with a young Athenian man who is about to notify the authorities that his own father had murdered one of his laborers. The dialogue will proceed, ultimately, to a conceptual exploration of what constitutes piety and justice. But Socrates is taken aback at first by Euthyphro's seeming betrayal of his own father. At the very outset of their discussion, instead of beginning with a thoroughgoing exploration of Euthyphro's worldview, Socrates, prematurely it seems, shares his conclusion about the correct moral stance in this case. He does so through a leading question posed to Euthyphro: "You are not afraid lest you too may be doing an impious thing in bringing an action against your father?"[1]

Leading questions can be useful for a hostile witness during a jury trial, or when trying to get a bloviating politician to come clean at a committee hearing, but they can be limiting and even destructive when applied in most work and personal contexts. Too often they come across as insincere and even manipulative. We all know when someone is shrouding an opinion or a directive in a closed-ended question, and we all can experience the temptation to go down this ill-conceived path at times. Closed-ended questions, almost by definition, limit what we may hear and learn from the other person. It's essential to take an intentional, careful, proactive stance toward open-minded listening and dialogue.

"Do you hate your job?" The response would likely be limited to yes or no (for all too many people, the answer is the former, accompanied by an eye roll or ironic chuckle).

When properly designed and delivered with a kind, genuine demeanor and tone of voice, open-ended questions create a safe and comfortable context in which people can express themselves freely. They foster an environment in which the interlocutor isn't saying what they think the other person wants to hear, but instead is speaking from the heart—perhaps delivering a difficult yet important message or a provocative point of view that's worth considering.

"What's been going on at work lately?" is an open-ended question that encourages the conversation partner to answer more deeply. The inquirer must be strong and confident enough to willingly and eagerly welcome contrary or even undermining replies. This mindset can open the possibility for creativity, innovation, and astonishing successes.

Socrates famously said that "the only thing I know is that I know nothing," and there is amazing power in not knowing. When we acknowledge and embrace the fact that our understanding and worldview are limited, we empower ourselves to learn and explore new paths that we never knew existed. It requires self-awareness and self-restraint to set aside what we think we know, our experience to date, and our expertise. We must pause and consciously put aside our assumptions. Embrace the unknown and unforeseeable. Take a counterintuitive stance. Even entertain radical notions of what is true and what might work.

This is as true in the daunting workplace of our day, with all its tactical and strategic complexities, as it was in ancient Greece, where Socrates and his fellow Athenians paused together in the agora to consider the mysteries of human existence. Think Talk Create ultimately transcends time, place, and circumstance.

A Portfolio of Good Questions

We once encountered a manager named Rick who desperately needed to learn the value of, and feel comfortable with, the Socratic wisdom of "not knowing." Rick worked as a professional manager for a private equity firm. He was hired by this private equity group, after a long executive career in technology, to resurrect one of the firm's portfolio companies, which had fallen on hard times.

During his first executive coaching session, Rick's energy and enthusiasm for growth were palpable, but he often got in his own way. He routinely shouted at team members, he couldn't and wouldn't tolerate deliberation, and he always positioned himself as having all the answers—so much so that Rick was known to call large team meetings, only to tell the team what was going to happen. He never asked for feedback, nor did he engage in dialogue. He simply told them what was going to happen and any suggestion about alternatives was met with frustration or a curt explanation as to why this other plan wouldn't work. To his great dismay, however, the portfolio company had yet to rebound after a few years with Rick at the helm.

Rick was reportedly an expert manager, and his take-no-prisoners leadership style was precisely the kind of shake-up this private equity company thought was needed for their struggling entity. His tour-de-force efforts and unusual knack for making employees cry had cultivated his image as a beastly CEO. But now he was stuck. Why would such a capable manager have trouble righting the course of a company that was sinking faster than a torpedoed ship? In Rick's case, it was based on an all-too-familiar thinking error.

Rick's colleagues wanted to develop new, innovative products in their effort to attract a shifting client base, but he became defensive and irritable when they came to him with new ideas. He'd quickly show his colleagues the door before even considering the creative proposals being presented to him; Rick seemed to think that he was the only one who could have a novel idea. Seeing him as a naysayer and all-around buzzkill, Rick's colleagues began to shelve new proposals. In other words, team members wouldn't even present their ideas to him because they were afraid of how he'd react. Most troublingly for Rick, his overseers at the private equity firm started to get frustrated. The portfolio company wasn't where it needed to be. To us, as outsiders looking in, it was all too clear why.

Rick had rarely paused for moments of self-reflection throughout the course of his career. He simply wasn't able to understand what was causing this company so much trouble. He lacked the ability to make collaborative decisions, and this mindset hardened over time because he thought his aggressive, know-it-all approach was what had gotten him to where he was in the first place. The truth of the matter was that Rick was indeed an incredibly smart guy. Sure, he bossed colleagues around, but he was as good or better than any high performer when it came to analyzing market trends. He went with his gut more times than not. He didn't always pick winners, but he batted over .500—and that success, coupled with his highly confident temperament, had served him well in his previous jobs. The problem was that now, as a CEO, this otherwise talented individual was a toxic presence. He literally did the opposite of Think Talk Create. Rick needed a new method.

Through a rigorous process of executive coaching over several months, Rick developed a more positive mindset and began to seek the input of others. His colleagues and his managers at the private equity company noticed a gradual improvement in his ability to engage with new ideas. The coaching process focused on helping Rick regulate himself well enough to stay calm, thoughtful, and open-minded. He learned mindfulness meditation so that he could stay grounded in the present moment, breathing deeply each time his mind moved toward stressed-out thoughts and disdainful expressions toward others. He practiced how to ask his colleagues open-ended questions: "What are the potential downsides of your proposal?" "What do you anticipate a customer could raise a concern about?" "How do you see the balance between potential financial benefits versus the research and development costs?" "Who else could weigh in on this complex proposal?" The questions were asked in

a true learning mode. They were not closed-ended or leading questions, with the right answers predetermined. Rick's
newfound expression of openness and humility was a profound transformation.

His colleagues and managers were beyond pleased. Team
members would laugh because, early on in this transformation, they could see the flicker in Rick's eyes when somebody
would present a competing idea; the old Rick was still in
there. But, to his credit, Rick worked really hard and kept at
it. Pretty soon, colleagues started to come to him with new
ideas instead of moving them to the trash bin. They would
look forward to meetings in which he would pose questions
instead of launching into a diatribe. Rick had turned himself
into a Think and Talk pro. He had positioned himself not
as an obstacle or a naysayer, but instead as a trusted partner.
Now he rarely needed to say no, because his questions were
so on point that team members could figure out whether
certain ideas were worth pursuing.

Pretty soon, the final step, Create, was added to Rick's
résumé. His active inquiry skills helped colleagues fine-
tune or revise new products as a group. And sure enough,
many of these new products were launched to market. Active inquiry didn't just create better feelings between Rick
and his colleagues, nor did it simply enhance the quality
of the workplace culture. It also had a direct effect on the
bottom line. People were no longer scuttling original ideas,
and Rick was no longer jamming his own ideas down their
throats. Instead, they were launching products developed in

a collaborative fashion. We glimpse here how Think Talk Create can be a key component to a business-growth strategy in our competitive, capitalist system.

Within the next year, Rick's portfolio company started to turn around. With a newfound sense of hope, Rick readily admitted that his old way of doing things wasn't of service as a CEO. Bullying is the kryptonite of innovation. He was amazed at how creativity skyrocketed when he started fostering a positive work environment. He was now building new products and services alongside his team members, and helping the company grow as a result.

Toward a Workplace Fit for Humans

How can we create the conditions that support Think Talk Create, empowering people like Jay and Rick to connect more powerfully with others and transform not only the way we do business but the way we live our lives? The best way to accomplish this is by thoughtfully and intentionally constructing environments where the unique force of a human being is valued and nurtured. Think Talk Create provides a road map for how to move in this direction, as Jay and Rick did so successfully. Their corporate environments fortunately provided them with enough freedom and flexibility to implement the methodology to the benefit of all.

But not all workplaces are so conducive. Many people work in environments that are so fast-paced and stressful as to deprive them of the time to slow down enough to get the

Think Talk Create process off the ground. When overworked and burdened by exacting requirements to hit their numbers quickly and continuously, people struggle to engage in the kind of self-reflection, conversation, and creative thinking that Jay did. Instead, they're stuck in a scared, intimidated, and self-defeating frame of mind. They understandably become exhausted and can have a short fuse, at times lashing out at others and diminishing their own credibility and influence. That was where Rick lived before embarking on executive coaching.

From the outset, Rick was a smart person attempting to navigate a pressurized work culture in which corporate success is ultimately determined by the bottom-line numbers. He lived in a near-constant state of denial about what actually contributed to professional success when working with a team. And Rick surely wasn't the only manager struggling in this way.

In the contemporary workplace, layers of pressure keep piling up for people at all levels, from individual contributors to middle managers to executives in the C-suite. People's bosses feel overwhelmed and in precarious situations with their own bosses, company board members, external customers, or regulators who are turning the screw. The emotions the company leaders experience are contagious and can propagate across teams and organizations, creating negative feedback loops and breeding a culture of fear and dysfunction. Research on social contagion shows that we are hardwired to respond to strong emotional states from others when we are exposed to them repeatedly. A boss or CEO under the gun will spread fear and anger across the company, sometimes breeding self-fulfilling prophecies of failure that are enough to cripple the business.

As the work environment comes to feel increasingly dehumanized, people are grasping at their own self-interest, acting like crabs in a barrel rather than bringing trust and empathy to their interactions. Psychological safety, the precondition for active inquiry and organizational growth, is hard to come by. Of course, psychological safety is not part of the law of the jungle or of the default, Hobbesian state of nature. Quite the contrary, psychological safety is the soaring achievement of a group of individuals who are calmly thinking, respectfully talking, and together creating a work culture that's suitable for human inhabitants.

The stories of Jay and Rick, and the companies that gave them the necessary freedom to perform their jobs humanely and well, provide beacons of hope in troubling times. In the next chapter, we'll explore how healthy and psychologically safe workplaces can reverse the dehumanizing trends of our day by ensuring that there's fertile ground for active inquiry and Think Talk Create.

2

BUILDING A CULTURE OF THINK TALK CREATE

The Whole Is Greater Than the Sum of Its Parts

A couple of years ago, we were invited to conduct a workshop during the annual conference of a property-management firm based in New England. Recent employee feedback indicated that a new problem had arisen, one that got the attention of the CEO. People were on record saying they didn't feel heard and that important information didn't always trickle upward. So the CEO sent us an invitation to facilitate a group retreat, where the whole range of employees could air their grievances and talk through how to improve the situation.

The banquet hall they had rented for the day was set along icy New England roads and was replete with faded salmon tones, gold light fixtures, and metal objects adorned with floral prints that the hall referred to as chairs. Describing them as uncomfortable would be an understatement.

To complicate matters, the space was preparing for a wedding or high school prom later in the evening, so tables were prearranged to make space for the dance floor and fabric was draped prettily along the bar. With no carnation on our lapels we were clearly out of place, but so were the scores of management professionals sitting with laptops and spreadsheets at the cloth covered, flower-laden folding tables.

The day had begun with several hours of tactical discussions about the siloed mentality that was hurting the company's performance. When the time came for us to take the stage, we could see the problem vividly displayed in front of us. Senior management talked over or at team members instead of talking *with* them. To make matters worse, business units were allocated to specific areas of the room, with all of the accountants seated at one table, property managers at another, social workers at a third, and so on. Several hours of discussion had not achieved any breakthroughs on what to do about the silo problem that was having such a negative impact on employees' quality of life and performance. The morning session, in fact, provided more evidence of silos, as each team coalesced around its tribal mentality. If the CEO's intent was to help each employee to develop a full-enterprise mindset—thinking of their individual roles as closely tied to the broader mission of the whole company—it clearly was not happening yet.

We began the workshop by engaging the room with some open-ended questions to develop a sense of trust and psychological safety. We posed questions like: "What are some things the company has done well recently?" and "How has the culture changed over the past few years?" But the cold New England weather seemed reflected in the crowd's demeanor. Comments were terse, and while we made some progress, the icy tracks had been laid and we were fighting an uphill battle from the start. Every response from the crowd was procedural, as though they were reading answers off a company spreadsheet or punch list. Nobody was willing to go off script and tell us what was really on their minds.

Frustrated that our attempt to engage this group in active inquiry was getting off to such a slow start, we pivoted to a different tactic. We paused and posed one of our favorite open-ended questions for a room full of anxious professionals fidgeting with their watches, hoping the hands will turn faster: "What keeps you up at night?" This question can take people aback at first, but it works so well because it prompts them to reflect on their fears and hopes—on what's most meaningful in their lives. In that moment, it felt as though the tide started turning. The employees, we hoped, were about to start inching away from their narrow focus on the operational challenges of each silo and take on deeper questions about what they really care about when they go to work.

In all of the years we have asked that question at company events, only once did somebody offer an immediate reply. "Nothing!" one person proudly shouted during a keynote address we were delivering. But upon further discussion, we quickly learned that this individual took a sleeping pill every evening before hitting the hay, and thus was seldom troubled by sleepless nights of anxiously staring at the ceiling and counting an unfathomable number of sheep. So, apart from this one medically induced Rip Van Winkle, the question always causes momentary silence from a crowd, as eyes dart down or up in thoughtful silence. It triggers contemplation.

This audience was no different. After a brief pause, predictable answers began emanating from the various tables, always reflecting whatever silo that group represented. The accountants said they were kept awake by gaps in the company's accounting software. The property managers lost sleep over the logistical issues of keeping their many buildings up and running. The lawyers were concerned with . . . well, everything. As we went around the room, each table mentioned something procedural, something quantitative and mathematical, something that dealt with zeros and ones or dollar signs. It was all numbers, all the time, until we reached the table way in the back where Hector Ortiz was sitting with his colleagues.

The Pickle Jar

Hector worked as a maintenance technician, and he sat at a table tucked in the back among his fellow custodians, many of whom were wearing blue shirts with white name patches, far away from the dance floor. Their appearance was in stark contrast to their colleagues at neighboring tables, who wore starched white shirts and neatly pressed blouses while manipulating digits on screens. The custodians worked with their hands, engaging with the actual smells and textures of the specific business they were in.

After we posed our open-ended question—What keeps you up at night?—and the higher-ups and professional staff had offered their predictable answers, Hector stood to offer a response that silenced the room. His answer perfectly encapsulated the empathy, trust, and collective values that are so vital to organizational well-being—and that none of the rest of them had thought to address.

Hector said his custodial pain point was "loss." The maintenance technicians serviced all of the assisted-living centers under the management company's portfolio. So, in addition to landscaping duties and exterior painting, these employees were also responsible for the interior upkeep of resident apartments. Every time a light bulb needed to be replaced or the garbage disposal became clogged, it was the custodian who dropped by to lend a hand. Given that many of the elderly residents lived alone, they welcomed these visits; to them, these custodians weren't just the hired help but friendly companions and, to a certain degree, family. Everyone in the room who was not a maintenance technician was shocked by the scope of Hector's work.

Hector shared the story of one resident, well into her nineties, who often asked him to perform additional odd jobs around the apartment, the most common assignment being to open a pesky jar of pickles. Over time, one pickle jar after another, they forged a human connection, a friendship that extended well beyond vinegar, salt, and water. They shared family stories, trivia answers from last night's *Jeopardy!*, and friendly well-wishes for the resident's never-ending parade of doctors' visits.

Hector never thought that by performing such handiwork he would become so emotionally invested in this relationship. But when the requests to open a pickle jar inevitably ceased, he was devastated. Each custodian around the table had a similar story, one of friendship and loss. Not one pain point from that group spoke to quantitative, logistical challenges; each custodian understood that the emotional connections to the residents were the most important aspect of their work.

After the custodians shared their stories, the floodgates at neighboring tables opened up. Seemingly everyone had something to share with similar humanistic concerns. The ensuing conversation was animated by an uncommonly human quality as the participants conceived, discussed, and created innovative solutions to their array of workplace challenges. It wasn't exactly clear what was going on, but it was obvious to everyone in the room that the group had never had an experience quite like it. Employees expressed gratitude to Hector, as well as the other custodians who had shared their experiences, for opening their eyes to a part of the company they'd never really thought about.

Once the stories got going, everyone started to talk across their silos. The legal group, always frustrated that property managers and social workers weren't quickly providing them with essential information to share with outside regulatory bodies, listened to what lay beneath the tardiness they resented. Whereas they'd previously thought that the employees in these other groups were lazy, or just didn't care, they now realized that they were actually overwhelmed due to problems with staffing following a couple of retirements and a maternity leave. So the different groups started trying to sort out which information the lawyers needed at what time and what information could reasonably be deferred.

Over the ensuing weeks and months, leaders and workers across the company reported that collaboration, productivity, and quality of life had increased substantially as a direct result of the program. One of the steps taken by this company after our seminar was the hiring of a grief counselor to speak with the custodians when they lost a customer or, more aptly, a friend. Through active inquiry and an emotionally transparent exchange of ideas, the company discovered a deeper truth together. Our follow-up interviews with seminar participants revealed that the Think Talk Create process seemed to be sticking, with a greater sense of psychological safety and openness to discussion at work. The company's success, however, was no accident.

We see these humanistic, nonquantitative concerns in virtually every organization we work with. People are seeking this connectivity, yet for some reason professional culture—which is ostensibly focused on efficiency and productivity—often unnecessarily and unknowingly gets in its own way. Through the emotional openness of one custodian, the property-management firm had actually stumbled upon the most powerful driver of organizational performance. That's because that day—in that poorly furnished room, set to host a wedding or prom—Hector showed his higher-status colleagues how to construct a psychologically safe environment.

Project Aristotle

Google's Project Aristotle was named in honor of the famous philosopher's notion that the whole is greater than the sum of its parts. For example, a brain and a foot and a hand and a heart are all interesting anatomical structures, but when put together (with a few other things, of course) you have a person. A human being is greater than the sum of all their body parts. The same can be said in business. With our property-management firm, the company was more than just the siloed departments sitting at separate tables.

Project Aristotle's findings have revolutionized the way organizations should think about the often problematic issue of "employee performance optimization"—how to ensure that individuals, and the teams they belong to, are performing at the highest possible levels.

Performance can mean many things. For some, performance might be measured by simple output calculations: Employee 1 manufactures twice as many widgets as Employee 2. But for other roles, especially those not on the production line, performance can be a tricky thing to assess. For example, how would you measure Hector's overall performance?

Google opted to reframe the concept of performance as "effectiveness" and considered, through a series of conversations with company leadership, what it actually means for a team to be effective.[1] Google's management acknowledged that, even at the center of the digital economy, just because one employee writes more lines of code than another does not necessarily mean that the former is more effective. Perhaps all that rapid code writing was allowing products to be released with an inordinate number of bugs. Perhaps the top coder created a hostile environment in which he was the only one who could concentrate.

Like the hyperaggressive hens that William Muir inadvertently bred, the quantitatively most productive individual is not necessarily the one you want in an organization aiming for long-term success. With humans as with hens, it's most fruitful to look at the characteristics of the team as a whole when assessing who's doing well.

Just like Indiana Jones searching for the Holy Grail, companies have taken varied paths in their attempts to increase the output and productivity of employees. Performance, some thought, was wholly dependent on compensation: employees could be motivated to perform at a higher level by incentivizing them with monetary rewards. Others believed that ratcheting up performance could be achieved through better office design and collaborative workspaces, open floor plans, aesthetically pleasing furniture, and nontraditional color palettes. Still others thought that better performance would result from carefully orchestrated, Hollywood-style casting, in which the strengths and character of one actor might supplement the strengths and character of another. In office settings, this might mean pairing one introvert with another introvert, or a senior manager with a future manager thought to have high potential.

Many believed that, in addition to salary and bonuses, employees could be incentivized through generous benefits and service programs, such as unlimited vacation time, on-site childcare, and subsidized lunch offerings. A handful even maintained that performance was solely the result of effective leadership—that only Napoleon, say, could have led his troops to victory, and that their (temporary) good fortune in battle was singularly determined by his extraordinary genius. Yet despite the pervasiveness of these commonly held notions, the Project Aristotle team found that all existing hypotheses were, in the words of one researcher, "dead wrong."[2]

Google's researchers knew there had to be some metric or measurable performance result in order to gather data, but instead of focusing strictly on the demands of those at the top, they sought feedback from three main tiers. For leadership at the executive level (the top), sales figures and product launches were two measurable and highly valued areas of critical insight. For team members in nonmanagerial roles, often referred to as individual contributors, what mattered most was culture. Middle managers, naturally enough, were in the middle of the spectrum, advocating for "both the big picture and the individuals' concerns saying that ownership, vision, and goals were the most important measures."[3] By engaging with employees up, down, and across the organization, researchers were able to paint a more complete picture of what effectiveness really means.

After examining over fifty years of organizational data that analyzed methods of boosting the effectiveness of teams, Google reached out to its global network of executives and identified 115 engineering teams and 65 sales units (180 teams in total), all of which had varying degrees of satisfactory annual performance. In other words, as in all organizations, some teams were better than others. The researchers had to include under-performers as well as over-performers to identify any potential missing ingredient in the recipe for organizational success. They wanted to see what the "good" teams had that the "bad" teams didn't.

Overall, Google's senior leaders had the general mindset that "building the best team meant combining the best people." Their view was similar to those who believed in central casting. Executives had often deployed this approach, but they also attached to it similar qualitative beliefs, such as that teams perform well if they socialize together outside of work and that relaxed dress codes can loosen the stuffiness of a traditional office setting. Employee benefits spanned the company hierarchy: Google even required that its subcontracted custodial staff receive health care and paid parental leave. It was this general hypothesis and approach—that the best teams equal the best people, supplemented by perks—that Project Aristotle set out to test. And test it they most certainly did.

Hundreds of interviews were conducted with team leads, while internal surveys were reviewed to gather data on over 250 items related to work-life balance and employee engagement. Shortly thereafter, Google being Google, the researchers applied numerous statistical models to unmask significant factors associated with employee performance. These factors were identified as relevant if they met three criteria: "(1) multiple outcome metrics, both qualitative and quantitative; (2) surfaced for different kinds of teams across the organization; and, (3) showed consistent, robust statistical significance."[4]

It was after carefully analyzing and discussing these statistical models that Project Aristotle began to present a clearer picture of what precisely contributed to unit effectiveness—or, more plainly, what made certain teams perform better than others. The researchers identified four supplementary and one principal marker of performance. The four that played a supporting role were well-known, popular sentiments: dependability, clarity/structure, meaning, and impact. These were everyday words in both personal and professional arenas. Dependability meant for the employees of Google what it means for a parent and child: to be reliable and accountable. So, too, did the concept of clarity and structure: goals and responsibilities were well defined and understood by the team. Meaning likewise meant significance, while impact meant that, in the eyes of employees, their work actually mattered.

But as we mentioned at the outset, the factor most closely associated with organizational performance, the one that far and away stole the show, was a concept little known outside academic circles: psychological safety. "Google's data," reported the *New York Times*, "indicated that psychological safety, more than anything else, was critical to making a team work."[5] Google's findings also confirmed reports that had been published only a few years prior in the *Harvard Business Review*. "High-performing teams aren't the result of happy accident. . . . They achieve superior levels of participation, cooperation, and collaboration because their members trust one another, share a strong sense of group identity, and have confidence in their effectiveness as a team."[6]

The methodology deployed by Google's researchers is a wonderful example of the necessary coexistence between the qualitative and quantitative realms. As indicated in their report, "Qualitative evaluations helped capture a nuanced look at results and culture but had inherent subjectivity. On the other hand, the quantitative metrics provided concrete team measures, but lacked situational considerations." It was these two forces working not in opposition but in unison that "allowed researchers to home in on the comprehensive definition of team effectiveness."[7] The "hard" and the "soft" were necessarily intertwined throughout. It's not a question of either/or, but of both/and.

Project Aristotle certainly relied a great deal on metrics and models, but they were metrics and models informed, funnily enough, by the Think Talk Create process. The researchers went to the many observed teams and asked open-ended questions to gather information about the essential ingredients of organizational performance. They were able to demonstrate the value of psychological safety by creating psychologically safe environments with the company teams, which in turn enabled Project Aristotle to be a success. The conclusion they reached was proven not only by their findings, but also somewhat subversively by the methods they used to reach their end. They had to think, talk, and create their way to a well-validated outcome.

In many respects, psychological safety can best be described as a sense or a feeling, a domain some Google staffers had never thought of in the context of teams. It's seldom a phrase at the tip of one's tongue, but we've all experienced its effect. In a business setting, psychological safety refers to an interpersonal dynamic in which each individual team member feels encouraged and empowered to share ideas and insights proactively, without trepidation or worry about negative judgment or disparagement. It was William Kahn, the

Boston University scholar, who first coined the term "employee engagement" and defined psychological safety in 1990 as "being able to show and employ one's self without fear of negative consequences of self-image, status or career."[8] More recently, Harvard Business School professor Amy Edmondson, a leading authority on psychological safety, wrote that the term "refers to a climate in which people are comfortable being and expressing themselves."[9]

This conceptual framework fit perfectly into what Google had discovered: "In a team with high psychological safety, teammates feel safe to take risks around their team members. They feel confident that no one on the team will embarrass or punish anyone else for admitting a mistake, asking a question, or offering a new idea."[10] You can probably remember a time in your career sitting around a conference table when you did not feel comfortable—ordinary social anxiety aside—sharing a helpful idea for fear of judgment or reprisal from a manager or colleague. Chances are you weren't the only person biting your tongue, so it should come as no surprise that, by inhibiting any dynamic exchange of ideas, psychologically unsafe environments stifle creativity and innovation.

Psychological safety is so powerful that, according to Elizabeth Necka, a researcher at the National Institute of Mental Health, patients battling addiction are statistically more likely to have positive health outcomes if they enjoy a transparent, trusting relationship with their health-care provider. It's so impactful that even in emergency situations, when patients are engaging with a provider that is likely not their own, their condition is still more likely to improve if the patient feels confident their doctor understands what they are going through at an emotional level. That is why psychological safety can be difficult to describe for those unfamiliar with the term. It's not one specific thing, like kindness. It's a culture or mood or sense. It's that willingness to speak up without fear of judgment or embarrassment.

Supplementing the research on psychological safety is the burgeoning body of research on the power of trust. Paul Zak, author of *Trust Factor: The Science of Creating High-Performance Companies*, has demonstrated the high correlation between trust in a workplace and economic performance.[11] Zak describes how the hormone and neurotransmitter oxytocin, usually associated with childbirth and breastfeeding, actually stimulates trust in humans and other mammals. He presents an experiment devised by Vernon Smith (a Nobel laureate in economics), in which a study subject is given a certain amount of money, which they can keep or give to a stranger, for whom the amount would triple. The stranger would then have the option of returning the favor by sharing some of the increase, perhaps half the total. But would they? The study subjects given the money in the first place had no way of being sure, but when several of them were given either oxytocin or a placebo via a nasal spray, the oxytocin group displayed a significant increase in their willingness to trust, thereby possibly increasing their net gain.

Companies cannot continually bathe their employees' brains with oxytocin, but, as Google's Project Aristotle reveals, creating an environment characterized by psychological safety can achieve the same kinds of positive outcomes. Emotional openness elevates oxytocin, which increases trust, which leads to further openness, and therefore more oxytocin and more trust. This creates the positive feedback loop known as a virtuous cycle—also known as a great working environment.

But even for "Don't Be Evil" Google, walking the walk is harder than talking the talk. In 2015, Google sat atop Glassdoor's "Best Places to Work" ranking, coming in at the coveted number-one spot. But just five years later, Google found itself outside the top ten looking in. The company had come under fire for what employees describe as a "crackdown" on the trusting culture that had once encouraged them to openly speak their minds. Per staff complaints, the company "recently canceled a regular series of company-wide meetings that allowed workers to pose questions to senior executives and began working with a consulting firm that has helped companies quell unionization efforts."[12]

In 2019, for example, Google disciplined employees who raised concerns about decisions made by company leadership pertaining to certain clients and work partners—decisions these employees felt were unethical. When management placed two staff members on leave for dissent, team members took to the streets to protest the decision. The act by leadership amounted to "brute force intimidation," said the employees, and it tarnished the reputation of Google as a bastion of humanity in the corporate world.[13]

Though not an exact science, Glassdoor's ratings are generated from employee reviews and consider a host of items, including compensation, benefits, culture, and senior management. Company intimidation tactics were one of the principal reasons cited for Google's slip.

If Google—the company that authored the report on how to optimize performance through the creation of psychologically safe environments—can let quantitative, bottom-line thinking get in the way of what they know to be best practice, anyone can.

Businesses need metrics and models, numbers and projections, calculations and data, analytics and aggregates. In short, businesses need math, but in our increasingly complex, globalized, twenty-first-century economy, they also need something that encourages us to step back and think about the big picture. We need to engage in meaningful dialogue and to reflect on data thoroughly enough to turn it into information, which can be translated into knowledge, which eventually can become wisdom, which can be exercised to create effective solutions. The ancient Greeks called this *phronesis*: the practical wisdom dependent on sound judgment, character, and habits. Sure, businesses need math, but they also need Think, Talk, Create.

As best-selling author Charles Duhigg wrote in the *New York Times*: "The behaviors that create psychological safety—conversational turn-taking and empathy—are part of the same unwritten rules we often turn to, as individuals, when we need to establish a bond. And those human bonds matter as much at work as anywhere else. In fact, they sometimes matter more."

Duhigg continued:

What Project Aristotle has taught people within Google is that no one wants to put on a "work face" when they get to the office. No one wants to leave part of their personality and inner life at home. But to be fully present at work, to feel "psychologically safe," we must know that we can be free enough, sometimes, to share the things that scare us without fear of recriminations. We must be able to talk about what is messy or sad, to have hard conversations with colleagues who are driving us crazy. We can't be focused just on efficiency. Rather, when we start the morning by collaborating with a team of engineers and then send emails to our marketing colleagues and then jump on a conference call, we want to know that those people really hear us. We want to know that work is more than just labor.[14]

A sense of feeling valued and respected, of permanence, and of knowing that he mattered is what empowered Hector to share with a room full of much higher-ranking colleagues what kept him awake at night. The sense of psychological safety began with equal treatment: the fact that Hector was not an outsourced contract worker but a part of the team, receiving the same employment status and benefits as his white-collar colleagues. It also came from equal access: the fact that Hector and the other custodians were invited to attend the annual company meeting and share their ideas. The company had laid the groundwork for an environment in which ideas could flourish, and that led to quantitative success. There's now a waiting list for all of their assisted-living facilities because of the incredible care provided by everyone, from the maintenance technicians to senior management.

It turns out that active inquiry isn't only a form of being nice to colleagues, but a disciplined methodology to understand the positions, motivations, and novel ideas of other team players. This information about the mental states of others is essential to achieving shared goals. The mere process of engaging in Think Talk Create, when done in a respectful and psychologically safe context, creates a genuine perception in others that we're open to their good ideas and eager for collaborative discussion and teamwork. Active inquiry allows others to feel heard and get on board with the team. As they experience a deepening of trust, they share more of their thought process—and once again we see the power of Think Talk Create as a rigorous activity that lays bare the truth. When we employ it skillfully, the temperature in the room comes down. Conversations become less heated and more harmonious, propelling the culture of the workplace to change for the better.

3

INSUFFICIENT EVIDENCE

*Gathering the Data That Too
Often Goes Missing*

Creating high-performing, psychologically safe workplaces—the kind that Project Aristotle demonstrated to be ideal—is an uphill battle. We have seen three workplaces that allowed for the Think Talk Create process to play out and yield positive results. Not all workplaces provide such fertile ground, unfortunately. People are often left to their own devices to find ways to infuse their basic humanity into a seemingly heartless, relentlessly numbers-driven work environment.

In workplaces that fall short of the ideal defined by Project Aristotle, people may suffer through day-to-day tasks burdened by a feeling that their assignments are disconnected from their personal experience and that their capacity to use good old-fashioned human judgment is disregarded, even disdained. At best, they are stressed and uncomfortable; at worst, they are fearful that their individual perspective and thought must be checked at the door, lest they come across as low performing, oppositional, or even a candidate for the chopping block. Stress and burnout are rampant in uncompromising work cultures that compel people to function in strict accordance with metrics, quarterly earnings reports, standard operating procedures, and algorithms. Groupthink often emerges from this mechanized mindset. No wonder the twenty-first-century workplace can leave so many people feeling depleted and demoralized.

Why is this the case? The answer largely stems from how our culture, especially since the nineteenth-century Industrial Revolution, has given pride of place to evidence-based science, often to an extreme. This scientific mindset has been applied in realms where it isn't quite fit for office, overreaching to the point where the complex human being becomes invisible in a sea of numbers and rigid protocols. Empirical science has been a blessing to our state of knowledge and quality of life in astonishing ways. But when it's rigidly misapplied in our multifaceted work lives, the blessing can quickly turn into a curse—at times, as we shall see, a lethal one.

When we consider the full complexity and variability of human experience and motivation, we might begin to suspect that behavioral science is more of an oxymoron than we'd care to admit. No matter how much science and technology try to slice and dice us, reducing people to productivity metrics or spending habits or numbers on a graph, finding predictability is a very tough assignment. Any time brain structures deep in the limbic system—the evolutionarily ancient center of emotion and instinct—are in play, all bets are off. We are far more than the sum of the parts examined by modern-day behavioral science. When people are reduced to their components and functional roles in work settings, a holistic view of complex human situations may be lost, frequently to the detriment of good long-term results— whether corporate profitability or ethical insurance settlements or clinical outcomes for ill patients.

There is an Indian parable that tells of a group of blind men feeling an elephant for the first time. One man feels the trunk and describes an elephant based on that limited experience; another feels a tusk and forms his description of the elephant based on the tusk alone. Another feels the foot, another the tail, and so on and so forth. The blind men all touch one small section of the whole but describe the elephant based on the section they touched. Applying this narrative to the modern workplace, who these days is able to touch and understand the entire elephant, not just delimited portions of its enormous body?

In a world dominated by empirical science and quantitative measurements of almost everything, we're constantly called upon to be evidence-based thinkers. We hardly question the role of evidence-based reasoning in science, engineering, or major business decision-making. The critical importance of careful analysis in these areas is clear and undisputed. Successful workers never play fast and loose with the truth when writing code, doing medical procedures, running a gel in the lab, or making a major financial investment. They thrive and depend on information and data analysis. They would consider it a grave dereliction of duty to work in any other way. Insufficient data can be deadly if we're doing surgery, launching a rocket, or designing an antilock-brake system for a car, which is why professionals in these endeavors employ such rigorous testing and multiple backups.

But we have trouble taking a similarly rigorous approach in the interpersonal space, where we have a powerful tendency to form snap judgments and take actions based on presumptions and deep misunderstandings about other people. It's remarkable how we tend to disregard evidence-based analysis when we enter into conversations that somehow, and quite misleadingly, strike us as informal, ordinary, or even beside the point. We almost never seek data about another person's inner life with the kind of rigor a scientist employs when seeking the more familiar type of quantitative data. But a lack of rigor with interpersonal engagement can be just as dangerous as we know it to be in our technical work.

In the interpersonal realm, where we struggle mightily at times to get along and collaborate with one another, an evidence-based approach is equally essential. The tactics for seeking sound and usable data in the social realm are, however, distinctive and very hard to master. People are often indirect, hidden, and guarded. They may not immediately say what's on their mind, either intentionally or because they don't themselves know what's going on inside, especially when strong emotions and stress are in play. A calm and psychologically safe space is foundational. Once that's in place, it takes disciplined, Socratic dialogue skills to pry the truth out of people and find common ground. Here is where active inquiry must come into play.

Most workers today, almost all of whom depend on varying types and degrees of technology to get their work done, agree with the general point that gathering and using data is essential. We almost never encounter people who don't want to think of themselves as evidence-based thinkers. It is, however, revelatory for them to see that active inquiry and the so-called soft skills that it leverages—such as curiosity about novel points of view, empathy, trust, and emotional intelligence—are equally evidence based. All of us—from scientists to physicians to business leaders to tech workers and beyond—should want to make decisions based on information, not ignorance. But our evidence-based skills are only partially complete if they lack attentiveness to self-awareness, calm conversations in a context of psychological safety, basic respect and civility, thoughtful listening, and a host of other interpersonal skills.

Active inquiry is not about touchy-feely conversations aimed simply at making others feel good. This isn't occasion for a kumbaya moment by any means. Instead, it's the sober recognition of the importance of a critical data-gathering tool. When we pause in our frenetic day-to-day activity and frame good open-ended questions that focus on authentic learning, surprising things can happen. Some examples of these questions in the workplace could be: What's your vision for this project? What are the risks versus benefits of this course of action? What's the timeline for this task in light of our other priorities? What's your level of buy-in here? Powerful dialogue often follows. Most obvious (but often overlooked) is that we actually learn something new from the other person. Our previous knowledge and assumptions may be constructively called into question—they may even be turned completely on their heads.

One's thinking widens and deepens when we listen closely to other people's replies to well-framed questions. High-level active inquiry can lead to divergent thinking, creativity, innovation, and growth. It can reveal the truth of what's meaningful to the other person, and thereby what is likely to be the most prudent and productive course of action. Recent research has shown that merely listening—regardless of what a person says in response to open inquiry—can lead to enhanced creativity; the effect is dependent on conditions of trust. A study on this topic demonstrated empirical evidence for the "mere listening effect on creativity and the mediating role of psychological safety."[1]

In health care, where one of us has worked for years, evidence-based medicine in the form of quantitative metrics is all the rage. But even in this increasingly technological field, humility is in order. Relying entirely on a widely used numerical rating scale can lead to disaster, as we are about to see.

Misleading Numbers, Loss of Life

Ramon, a young sous-chef, had not been happy for a very long time. He'd withdrawn from friends and family members so thoroughly that most of them had stopped reaching out to him. He quit playing for the adult soccer team he'd long enjoyed because it took all the energy he could muster just to hang on to his job at a local bistro. He worked hard, but for more than a year he hadn't done much else.

Ramon knew that things were getting serious when he started missing work. He'd never called in sick, but now he did so two or three times each week. When he was still with his girlfriend and he couldn't bear to face the day, she'd rouse him out of bed, push him into the shower, and get him out the door. But then his irritability and foul moods drove her away.

Then Ramon began to hear voices taunting him for being such a failure. These voices also told him to throw himself into oncoming traffic.

Not since he was a teenager struggling with academic problems and a breakup with a high school girlfriend had Ramon thought of ending his life. Now self-harm was becoming an obsession. He started slicing his left wrist with a razor, watching the blood ooze, and noticing both the pain and the relief. Instead of cutting deeper, though, Ramon texted his brother-in-law, who picked him up and drove him to the emergency room.

Ramon had taken antidepressant medication in high school, but when he graduated and went on to a culinary institute his mood improved, so he stopped the drug regimen. For the next fifteen years, Ramon generally felt and functioned pretty well. He had many friends, went on lots of dates, and enjoyed the company of others. Despite the stress of restaurant work, he'd risen in his job to having a prominent and respected role, as well as an impressive salary. But then his thoughts turned increasingly hopeless and morbid. After a while, he asked himself, "Why go on this way?" He no longer saw any meaning or value in everyday existence, and death looked like the only hope for relief.

Once he was in the hospital, though, Ramon was surrounded by kind, earnest clinicians who seemed zealous about helping him. Despite his trepidations about side effects and overall skepticism, he agreed to go back on medication. Actually, he found that decision to be as absurd as the rest of his life, but he went along with the doctors' recommendation of an antidepressant called citalopram. Because of the auditory hallucinations that berated him, his doctors also prescribed an "atypical antipsychotic" called aripiprazole, meant to quell hallucinations and enhance the effectiveness of citalopram.

In Ramon's case, the treatment addressed his symptoms remarkably well, just as it does in about 60 to 70 percent of depressed individuals who take those same medications. For Ramon's clinicians, this improvement was no surprise. It was merely confirmation that the best practice is evidence-based medicine, in which well-defined treatment algorithms and decision trees guide clinical decision-making. Instead of imperfect, subjective clinicians relying on their personal impressions and potentially biased judgments to determine the proper course of treatment, a clearly defined scientific process becomes the overriding metric.

In medical research studies and in routine clinical care, psychiatrists often quantitatively rate the severity of a patient's depression using numerical scales, assessing such factors as sad mood, feelings of guilt, weight loss, insomnia, inability to work, anxiety, agitation, and suicidal thinking. The goal of hospital treatment is to reduce the numbers on a measure such as the seventeen-item Hamilton Depression Rating Scale (HAM-D), to see suicidal thinking and planning disappear. Ramon's HAM-D score was in the severe range at thirty-two when he was first admitted to the hospital. By the time he left, it was down to seven. The resolution of his clinical depression was obvious and substantial because those HAM-D numbers looked great. By all objective measures, his treatment had been a life-saving success and was cause for celebration. The only problem was that, less than seventy-two hours after he was discharged from the hospital with hugs and high fives all around, Ramon killed himself.

Given that we all keep so many of our thoughts and feelings private, it's usually difficult or impossible to discern in retrospect why exactly a person commits suicide. In hindsight, though, it was obvious that Ramon's morbid thoughts and recent self-injurious actions were more relevant than the numbers on a widely accepted rating scale. The field of psychiatry, in its eager embrace of all things quantitative, may be overestimating the validity and reliability of some of its own trusted tools. Ramon's treatment team's overreliance on the HAM-D calls to mind the all-too-common Dunning-Kruger effect (described by research psychologists David Dunning and Justin Kruger in the 1990s): a cognitive bias toward greater confidence in one's skills than is warranted.

Because of human individuality and emotional complexity, active inquiry needs to be deployed at the outset (or at least in the early stages) of almost any professional, business, or personal interaction. This data-gathering technique is the only way for us to make truly evidence-based decisions, which means relying on all the evidence, not just the numbers.

In medicine, there's a well-established protocol for this kind of evidence gathering. Whenever there's a devastating and unanticipated outcome like Ramon's, medical teams conduct a postmortem analysis in a forum that many hospitals call morbidity and mortality (M&M) conferences. In order to promote honest discussion, what gets said at these conferences is considered "confidential peer review" and as such is protected from legal action, which makes the M&M sessions the perfect example of active inquiry incorporated into a work process. These discussions empower physicians to ask each other the hard questions and speak with complete honesty. By sealing off everything as confidential and legally privileged, the process gives doctors the latitude to engage in free-flowing back-and-forth that can generate critical insights—and ideally lead to quality improvements in the future. As a group of caregivers, they inquire without prejudice into the uncensored and brutal truth.

The tragedy is that doctors sometimes engage in this form of active inquiry only after things have gone terribly wrong. Our point in this book is that they, like all other professionals working in teams, need to incorporate this kind of analysis up front, even as they plan their first steps.

In the aftermath of Ramon's death, the post hoc M&M process underscored the value of active inquiry even more explicitly. The doctors concluded that the most significant factor contributing to Ramon's suicide was likely the dearth of active inquiry during his clinical care.

What had been missed in all of the conversations with him over the course of his weeks in the hospital? How might the treatment team have gathered more accurate and relevant information? What were the collective blind spots that resulted in everyone thinking that Ramon's ostensible recovery was genuine? How had each member of the team become so convinced of Ramon's improvement, in spite of everything he had told them about how dark his thinking had been recently?

There was no suicide note to help clarify the course of events, so Ramon's mindset and decision-making process would forever remain shrouded in mystery. But one thing was crystal clear: his observable symptom reduction and the numerical changes on his HAM-D belied his inner thoughts and final actions. His clinicians, who were just trying their best to integrate their clinical judgments and an imperfect rating scale, had missed the entire thing. It was a classic death by numbers.

It's possible that the antidepressant medications had contributed to reducing Ramon's depression, as reflected on the HAM-D. But since antidepressants often infuse a person with more energy, they may have also given him just enough drive to act on his hopelessness and actually end his life. It's also plausible that Ramon felt relieved and emboldened when, during his hospital stay, he settled on a definitive plan that he would kill himself soon after getting home. Assured by this decision that he wouldn't have to suffer much longer, perhaps he felt freed from his demons and glimpsed light at the end of the tunnel. Now, maybe, he could relax, laugh, and enjoy his final moments with the friendly staff members at the hospital.

Not surprisingly, a patient's inner drama can be hidden to clinicians who only get to know them for a short period of time. A doctor's main job is to assess their patients' clinical status on the basis of observable signs and focused interviews about symptoms (and then provide evidence-based treatment accordingly). This is how mental health professionals are required to practice in the research-driven, quantitative era in which we live. Training programs, as well as continuing education programs for more experienced clinicians, focus predominantly on building this skill set. Insurance plans, both private and public, pay only for evidence-based treatment. If a clinician needs to spend extra time with a patient like Ramon to explore his mindset more deeply and try to uncover novel approaches that might support his recovery, the insurance coverage for that service is likely to be limited or nonexistent.

It's also true that in the caring professions, where we might expect individuals to be most compassionate, workers are facing stress and burnout themselves. This does not create an atmosphere conducive to calm exploration enhanced by open-ended conversations.

The vast majority of mental health professionals are insightful, empathetic, and mission driven. They pursued this career path not to become wealthy or famous, but to form meaningful connections and therapeutic alliances with vulnerable people. They tend to be idealistic and deeply committed to their mission, but everyone has a breaking point. Under the pressures of modern-day health care, it's not surprising that clinicians aim to get as much objective information from patients as quickly as they can. They need to efficiently document their findings in the medical record, both to meet regulatory requirements and to ensure that the hospital receives payment for the services. The only way to get through a harrowing workday is to use lots of closed-ended questions, which evoke a simple yes-or-no reply but not necessarily the truth.

Clinician: Are you feeling safe today?
Ramon: Yes, definitely.

Clinician: So the suicidal thoughts have resolved?

Ramon: Yes, they're gone.

Clinician: Is there anything else we can do to help you at this point?

Ramon: No thanks, I'm ready to go home.

Mainstream psychiatry might learn a lesson and consider a remedy from crisis hotlines that serve suicidal individuals and others who feel they're at the end of their rope. A leader in the movement toward open-ended, non-judgmental dialogue is Samaritans, a nonprofit organization founded in England following World War II and exported to the United States in 1973. Its prime mover was Monica Dickens, the great-granddaughter of Charles Dickens, who may have done more than anyone to increase empathy for the plight and desperation of working people in Victorian England. Ms. Dickens presided over the establishment of the first US chapter of Samaritans in the towering Arlington Street Church, by the Public Garden in Boston, in 1973. She followed up with the opening of the second chapter of Samaritans on Cape Cod in 1977. The organization now has a strong presence in the northeastern region of the United States, providing crisis services as well as public educational programs and support groups for people who have lost loved ones to suicide.

Calm, respectful dialogue has always stood at the core of the Samaritans methodology. For decades, Samaritans has functioned as a telephone service that suicidal individuals could call and speak to another human being about their plight; in recent years, the organization has also added texting services to cater to the communication predilections of the younger set. Volunteers man the lines and foster respectful, open conversations with callers to support them in finding solutions other than ending their own lives. In a matter of minutes, highly trained and skilled Samaritans volunteers facilitate the type of active inquiry that Ramon might have benefited from during his psychiatric hospitalization.

In retrospect, could the tragic death of Ramon have been prevented? The treatment team had acted in accordance with the contemporary standard of care. The clinical use of more open-ended questions in sessions might have given him a fighting chance, though of course we could never claim definitively that it would have altered the outcome. But what if one or more of his clinicians had taken an extra twenty or thirty minutes to sit with him and have a free-ranging discussion? They might have avoided or de-emphasized closed-ended questions, which are more suited to checklists and rating scales than deep, meaningful conversation. What if they had engaged in active inquiry by asking Ramon questions like these: Where do you see yourself in one year, or five? What are a couple of things you're most looking forward to doing now that you're well? Who are the people in your life that are most worth staying alive for? Who will you tell if you start feeling hopeless and suicidal again?

If active inquiry had been rigorously employed as the linchpin of Ramon's clinical care, perhaps his clinicians would have picked up signs that things weren't as copacetic as his HAM-D numbers suggested. Perhaps they would've noticed hesitation, darting eyes, shifting, or other telltale signs that Ramon was not quite as well as they thought. Asking powerful questions and attending closely to the responses, both verbal and nonverbal, is at the heart of sound clinical care. Sigmund Freud noted that we can get a glimpse of people's underlying emotional world if we pay attention to their nonverbal expressions. The unconscious is ultimately irrepressible. "If his lips are silent, he chatters with his fingertips," Freud wrote. "Betrayal oozes out of him at every pore."[2]

Slowing down, asking the right questions, listening, and observing—the active inquiry process might have allowed Ramon's treatment team to discern an underlying problem and take more productive action, such as delaying his discharge from the hospital until a stronger safety plan was in place.

Now, here's one more example from the medical world, revealing the potentially detrimental tunnel vision of experts who attend exclusively to neuroscience and leave active inquiry out of the equation.

What the Savant Didn't See

Dr. C. Miller Fisher was the godfather of twentieth-century neurology. His accomplishments include the first identification of transient ischemic attacks, the precursors to strokes, and the discovery that coronary artery plaques are a frequent source of stroke. These were fundamental contributions to clinical practice. But even such an éminence grise commanding the world's latest technology could still miss the subtleties of what was going on in any given individual's subjective experience. That's why multiple points of view, brought to bear in a free and open exchange, are so important.

In the early nineties at Massachusetts General Hospital— in a unit that bore Fisher's name, no less—the great doctor ran a weekly two-hour conference, during which he would interview a single patient in front of awestruck medical students. Not only had the service been named after Fisher, but just behind him hung a large oil painting that depicted the great neurologist exactly as he appeared in the flesh. The students could hardly believe they were in the presence of this aging deity, a medical hero of a different era. Even though Fisher was as polite and refined as he was brilliant, he made it clear that these students were there as silent observers, not participants. There would be no naive observations or dumb questions from kids in short white lab coats.

One day, the patient was a middle-aged man stricken with abulia—a syndrome of apathy, indifference, flat facial expression, and lack of spontaneous speech or social engagement. He'd suffered a stroke, confirmed by an MRI, in a deep brain structure that, when damaged by a lesion, leads predictably to the symptoms he presented.

It took a gargantuan effort for this man to muster a one- or two-word answer to Fisher's most basic questions. Can you move your right hand? "Yes" (and the patient slowly demonstrated with a gentle fist clench). Can you remember when you came into the hospital? "Last week." What did you have for breakfast this morning? "Eggs." Then an excruciating, utter silence. The man's motor functioning was intact. He reacted in the expected way to a reflex hammer. Sensory functions also were intact, with the patient responding to gentle pinpricks on both arms and legs. But his personality and social connectedness were shot. He hardly looked around the room, and he seemed utterly indifferent to what was going on. There was no small talk; he elaborated on nothing. It was a brutal two hours in that conference room, but Fisher's pedagogy was brilliant—every known symptom of abulia (along with what was not affected by abulia) was laid bare.

But there was one thing, maybe the critical piece of the story—and still a mystery today—that Fisher missed entirely. Had he opened the room to questions and observations from the students, who knows if anything more would have emerged during the formal session. In any event, Fisher never had the chance to see what happened right after his carefully orchestrated demonstration ended. A medical student began to wheel the patient back to his bed. But just outside the conference room, the student paused for a moment, then leaned down to make eye contact and ask a simple question: "How was that for you?"

This mild-mannered patient, so flattened by his stroke, looked up expectantly. His eyes brightened and his smile slowly widened until he looked almost ebullient. In defiance of all the well-established laws of abulia, the usual constraints of this man's condition were being overridden by something deeper, a force humming along beneath the stroke and contradicting all the MRI readings and precise, quantitative metrics. Although this patient had appeared entirely indifferent to anything going on around him, it turned out that he was acutely aware of, even amused by, one thing he noticed on the wall behind the great doctor throughout the interview. In response to the medical student's gentle, open-ended question, he opened his mouth and said with great enthusiasm, "That's quite a portrait of Dr. Fisher!"

Quantum physics, which incorporates and yet transcends Newtonian physics, tells us that we cannot measure a phenomenon without fundamentally changing it. In 1927, physicist Werner Heisenberg introduced this key insight as the "uncertainty principle." Dr. Fisher's interview laid bare the mechanics of abulia. But the conference itself, with a human observer studying the phenomenon of abulia, actually changed what abulia is, rendering it less clear-cut than the textbooks suggest. A doctor influences a patient's blood pressure when she induces anxiety by measuring the patient's blood pressure—the classic "white-coat effect." Just so, Fisher—both in the flesh and in the oil painting—changed the basic nature of the patient's abulia, likely by tweaking his limbic system and evoking a powerful emotion. By "measuring" the abulia—the hallmark of which is apathy—Fisher had transformed the patient's experience into the exact opposite.

Fisher, the expert, knew full well that the patient had stroke-induced abulia, so all his clinical queries during the two-hour session had been leading questions—each reply a foregone conclusion, a closed loop to confirm Fisher's extensive knowledge. And so it was left to the student, outside the bounds of the case conference, to ask an open-ended question that didn't have a preordained response and couldn't be answered with a yes or no. The med student's simple, empathetic inquiry may have done more to propel this patient toward recovery than any high-tech approaches available at Mass General.

Talk Before You Leap

Any activity—treating patients, teaching students, managing employees, policing tough neighborhoods, leading soldiers into combat—can overlook what's most fundamental, which is the full complexity of each individual, and along with it, their full potential to succeed and contribute. In too quickly resorting to empirical science and quantitative modeling, we can overlook what's right before us and miss opportunities we may never realize existed. This is as true in neuropsychiatry as it is in personal relationships, business negotiations, military strategy, and journalism. The disciplined approach of active inquiry provides the method for mastering the skill to nurture open-ended conversations, which can take you to the heart of the matter. It protects us from digging unnecessary holes for ourselves and others as a result of making assumptions based on incomplete evidence and jumping to conclusions prematurely.

Without active inquiry (and without a good editor) a reporter might take what one person tells her at face value and write a story that gets it all wrong, saddling her newspaper with a costly lawsuit and getting herself fired. That's why good newspapers require multiple sources to confirm the truth. A salesperson can make a great pitch—so airtight and well thought-out that the customer simply can't say no—but miss the fidgeting that betrays the reality, which is that the potential customer still has doubts. The salesperson, believing she has said all that needs to be said, fails to pause and ask what the customer thinks and feels. No deal. Behavioral economics has taught us that people make decisions less on the basis of rational analysis than on the basis of social, emotion-driven considerations. That's why questions confined by the expectation of a yes-or-no answer so often miss what's really going on. That's also why situations, like Dr. Fisher's demonstrations, in which experts or senior people have no interest in hearing what others have to say so often miss the diagnosis, as well as the cure.

Active inquiry, on which the entire Think Talk Create process relies, shouldn't be an afterthought or a matter of happenstance. If it isn't employed proactively and early on, we run the risk of coming to ill-informed and incomplete conclusions. The clinical narratives in this chapter reveal how lost opportunities—or, in a worst-case scenario, death—may result from neglecting to deploy active inquiry throughout a diagnostic process and treatment. Active inquiry in the case of Ramon and the patient with abulia only came into play after the key interactions: in one case in an M&M review, and in the other case with a med student asking a simple, human question after a conference run by an expert. It's worth reflecting on what might have been different for these individuals if active inquiry had been incorporated in a systematic manner from the outset. In the chapters to come, we will also look at how active inquiry—or the lack thereof—can be a major determining factor in the success or failure of careers, businesses, communities, and even the future of life on earth.

4

BLINDED BY BEING RIGHT

Overcoming the Trained Incapacity of Experts

For many experts like Dr. Fisher, analytical reasoning and scientific know-how are über-developed—potentially at the expense of other skills. Their meticulous attention to technical details appears at times to interfere with having an appreciation of the seemingly mundane. Fisher's profound understanding of abulia actually may have been the greatest impediment to his noticing the patient's preserved capacity for emotional expressiveness. It was a classic case of missing the forest for the trees: a laser focus on brain lesions, impaired neural pathways, and symptoms shrouded the unanticipated demeanor of the patient when circumstances shifted.

Sociologist Thorstein Veblen, in 1933, called this phenomenon "trained incapacity" and described it as "that state of affairs whereby one's very abilities can function as blindness."[1] It may, as we've seen, result in overlooking key information about a patient. Another distressing manifestation of this process for patients may be a doctor's lack of bedside manner, when the doctor's technical skills are unquestioned but there's a disturbing lack of empathy and human connection. Trained incapacity can plague experts not just in clinical medicine, but really in any area of contemporary work.

Founder's Syndrome

After a full year of floundering, a software entrepreneur named Brad realized he had a big problem at work. He reached out for executive coaching to help understand what he could do to fend off a brewing storm, but he never followed through to schedule an appointment. This is not an uncommon scenario in the coaching world, since we are all prone—especially when we're "too busy"—to avoidance of disturbing emotions and potential challenges to our basic (often overinflated) views of ourselves. By the time Brad reached out again, it was too late. The company he'd helped to cofound, with three longtime friends and collaborators, had let him go. He was overwhelmed, confused, and angry. An initial conversation with him showed that he was full of blame and resentment. How could they remove a cofounder, and a top-tier technical expert in a cutting-edge field, from his own firm? The software company, now highly profitable and employing over seventy-five people, had clearly changed and left Brad in the dust, and he was ashamed and humiliated by the bold coup that had been perpetrated against him. One of the other cofounders didn't mince words when telling Brad, on his way out the door, that he had succumbed to "founder's syndrome"—Brad's problematic attitude that he could act however he wanted in a maturing company, just because he was partly responsible for launching it in the first place.

Part of Brad's negotiated severance package was to work with a coach to help him navigate his career transition. He wanted to understand what had happened and plan for how he could prevent such a cataclysmic failure going forward. He also wanted to explore what kind of job might be suitable for him in the future. He agreed to engage in a postmortem, 360-degree assessment in which the coach would interview a half dozen of his colleagues about his strengths, weaknesses, and areas to improve in order to develop his career in a positive direction. The coach would openly and nonjudgmentally ask his former colleagues—in accordance with the active inquiry method—what they had observed and why they'd determined that Brad needed to go. In many ways, it was similar to the M&M conferences physicians use, but in this case it was to understand the cause of death for Brad's job.

The feedback from each person interviewed was essentially the same. Brad was brilliant, hardworking, tenacious, and committed to the highest professional standards for himself and the firm. He was highly respected for his quantitative reasoning skills; nobody in the company was more mathematically or technically adept. But he had a fatal flaw:

he didn't listen. In conversations with people up, down, and across the organization, Brad always came across as already knowing the answer. He cut people off mid-sentence, rolled his eyes, tensed his shoulders, and generally made it clear that he wasn't absorbing anything they had to say. It didn't help that he was someone who, according to his coworkers, "never smiled"—even when he had good personal reason to do so, or after someone shared happy news or made an amusing quip in a meeting. Brad generally came across as humorless, robotic, even intimidating.

Executive coaches try to deliver feedback in an honest and uncompromising manner while softening the ego blow with reassurances (realistic ones, of course) that enhancing insight and self-awareness can propel progress. Brad heard many direct quotes from his colleagues when he was debriefed, and some of it was harsh. "The whole time I'm talking," one of his colleagues said, "he's trying to cut holes in what I'm saying—and he doesn't really want me to succeed." Another highly accomplished colleague and peer made the blistering observation that Brad "reduced me to being a glorified secretary." Another remarked that "the vitality in the company has gone way up since he left."

Brad could hardly believe what he was hearing. He reacted with scorn, becoming defensive and dismissive. "They just don't get it," he said. "All I was doing was working hard to help the company."

Before this 360 evaluation, there was no forum for people to express how they were affected by Brad's temperament, but in fact there had been plenty of ominous interpersonal cues that Brad didn't notice. He failed to appreciate the significance of the fact that he had been excluded from key meetings scheduled without his input. As the situation deteriorated, Brad never paused to reflect on why people were actively avoiding him. Instead, he fumed about the slights, becoming even more judgmental and controlling. At the meetings in which he was included, people clammed up as he barked orders about what each of them needed to get done on his projects.

Like so many of us, Brad struggled mightily to slow himself down enough to absorb the powerful messages, verbal and nonverbal, that people were trying to convey. His colleagues felt that they never could be honest with him about how diminished, demeaned, and stifled they felt when working with him. The workplace had become toxic when he was around. In a nutshell, Brad was contributing to an atmosphere that was the exact opposite of the psychologically safe, collaborative work environment that Project Aristotle demonstrated to be optimal for strong team performance. Brad paid a very high price for his trained incapacity, eventually being hung out to dry by his longtime colleagues. What could he do to improve things going forward?

Frontal Lobe

There has been a growing understanding over the last few decades that attention deficit disorder in adults is a

biologically based condition, often but not always presenting initially in childhood, that degrades a person's sustained
focus on tasks such as reading and completing projects. The
lack of attentional control often manifests itself in impaired
executive functions: planning, reasoning, problem-solving,
decision-making, and cognitive flexibility. The disorder is
treatable with medications—such as Ritalin—but it is not
purely biological. Its severity is usually determined by the
nature and difficulty of the task at hand, as well as by socio-
cultural expectations. It becomes a clinical disorder when it
gets in the way of social and occupational functioning and
the individual seeks psychiatric help to manage the troubling symptoms.

Brad's mental focus and sustained attention to work
tasks were strong, and there was no indication that he
had diagnosable attention deficit disorder. But he suffered
with a related and deeply problematic—though still under-
recognized and unnamed—condition that we might label
"active inquiry deficit disorder." Active inquiry—rooted in
open-ended questions, attentive listening, and powerful
dialogue—can be understood as the supreme function of
the frontal lobe, the region of the brain that subserves executive functions. It allows us to bring a holistic perspective—
with wisdom, social intelligence, and empathy—to human
relationships and problem-solving. This was the key set of
skills that Brad didn't have and that he didn't even realize he
needed in order to succeed in a complex and growing company where collaboration is as essential as technical ability.

In our frazzled and frenzied times, when the stress of always being busy and needing to get things done supersedes unstructured time and thoughtful dialogue, active inquiry deficit disorder has become part of our way of life. Bosses push their employees to the limits of their capabilities, creating risks of reduced job performance and burnout. A myopic focus on short-term profits, as reflected on quarterly profit-and-loss statements, sacrifices a view of long-term plans for sustainable growth. Parents rush their children from one scheduled activity to the next (youth sports, dance classes, violin lessons, playdates) without slowing down enough to connect with their children about what they're actually thinking and feeling. And then there's the ubiquitous and ever-worsening set of problems presented by social media.

Social media tempts us with user-friendly platforms for spouting opinions, and the half-baked gets a lot more play than the carefully considered—by design. The fact that users don't have to deal with face-to-face responses to their comments normalizes bullying and denigration, and the electronic back-and-forth replaces genuine, sustained interaction. Filtering algorithms favor outrageous clickbait over well-documented arguments. In his testimony before Congress in 2020, Amazon CEO Jeff Bezos called social media "a nuance-destruction machine."[2]

In fact, Facebook, Twitter, and most other social media platforms foster the very antithesis of active inquiry, and their ascendency has coincided with the obliteration of such traditional venues for open-ended conversation as the family dinner table and the leisurely business lunch (Brad certainly went out for lunches, but they could never be described as "leisurely"), where the purpose is to form long-term, mutually beneficial alliances. With the digital efficiency clock ticking away, we're intent on meeting the deadline and closing the deal right now, without really laying the groundwork for a deeper understanding of the issues at play. Similarly, in the age of electronic media, politics has devolved into delivering snappy sound bites, disingenuously staking out positions locked in place by focus groups and polling, and talking over, past, and through one another. Actual debates intended to air competing viewpoints and perhaps arrive at a workable compromise have gone the way of straw boaters and ladies who lunched in white gloves.

If the essence of active inquiry is simply asking and listening, why is it so hard to get it right? Is it really so difficult to ask other people open-ended questions that are agenda free and nonjudgmental? Shouldn't it be easy to hear their responses and engage with them in civil, productive dialogue? It requires, as we have seen, immense patience and self-restraint. For hard-drivers like Brad, it can be extremely difficult to discipline oneself to remain grounded in the moment, inquiring and listening. The primary hurdle is that active inquiry requires the presence of two or more calm, well-focused brains functioning in a healthy state of almost Zen-like repose. If even one of those brains is flooded by stress hormones or an imbalance in neurotransmitters, frontal lobe functioning deteriorates and the likelihood of active inquiry evaporates.

In order to get a glimpse of what happens here, it's worth considering the most extreme version of frontal lobe dysfunction and thinking about how it bears on more common situations like Brad's. In the study of neurobiology and brain science, the classic illustration of what we'd be without a healthy frontal lobe is Phineas Gage, a steady, pleasant, and upstanding construction foreman who was, essentially, transformed into a completely different person by a freak accident.

In September 1848, Gage was leading a crew clearing a roadbed for the Rutland and Burlington Railroad near Cavendish, Vermont. Much of their work consisted of blasting rock, which involves boring a hole deep into an outcrop, adding blasting powder and a fuse, and then using a three-foot-long tamping iron to pack sand or clay into the hole above the powder to contain the blast and direct its energy back into the granite.[3]

Toward the end of the day, Gage was pressing down on the tamping iron when he looked over his right shoulder and opened his mouth to speak. Just then, the tamping iron sparked against the rock, ignited the powder, and blew the thirteen-pound steel rod through his upper jaw, his left eye, the left side of his brain, and out the top of his skull, landing eighty feet away. A handful of brain tissue traveled with it.

Miraculously, Gage survived. In fact, these massive injuries did nothing to cause widespread brain damage; movement and sensation—including hearing, speaking, and seeing—were left perfectly intact. What it did do was obliterate his frontal lobe. Gage's syndrome was an extreme but instructive version of what Brad suffered at work when his anatomically intact yet vulnerable frontal lobe was bathed with stress hormones and receiving rapidly firing inputs from the brain's fear center.

Gage was a changed man after the brain injury, with a whole new—and profoundly disturbing—set of personality traits. Although he could still see and hear and perform physical activities, he turned into an ill-tempered individual who raged, swore, and drank. He no longer had any way of governing the interplay of emotion and intellect, impulse versus well-considered ideas. In his straitlaced New England community, this behavioral disinhibition meant that he could no longer maintain gainful employment, and he became a pariah. Years after he died in 1860, his body was exhumed for medical study. His skull and the infamous tamping iron are on view at Harvard Medical School to this day.

During most of human evolution, when the wiring of our brains took shape, survival favored decision-making that was based on instinct and intuition: fast, automatic, and unconscious. This is what economist and Nobel laureate Daniel Kahneman calls "system 1" thinking. It requires very little energy expenditure because it's so rapid and reflexive—more like pulling your hand back from a hot stove than carefully weighing the pros and cons of doing so. The frontal lobe, which grew to its current size much later in the evolutionary process, has little or no role to play in system 1.[4]

When a poisonous snake is about to strike, there's no need to pause, reflect, and consider long-term consequences or the big picture in terms of the common good. Quite the contrary. Without a quick, instinctive response, the most likely consequence of an angry snake will be strictly short-term: you'll get bitten and die.

But further along in human evolution, the threats and challenges became more subtle and complex, with other people often serving as the cause of the threats but, para-doxically, even more often providing the safety we needed. Adding to the challenge (and the level of chronic stress) was the fact that both the existential threats and the life-preserving systems of social support could persist for years, if not a lifetime.

To negotiate these complex, long-lasting relationships, humans needed to avoid the obvious threats and form protec-tive alliances. In this situation, system 1 thinking—especially its fight-or-flight, adrenaline-driven variation—did not provide a sufficient repertoire of responses. This is why the frontal lobe has evolved to such an incredible extent, consol-idating the functions of the executive brain to help us modu-late fear responses, defer gratification, and otherwise perfect the give-and-take that social life among humans requires. Even so, our more primitive, all-or-nothing brain structures and their knee-jerk responses were never replaced. Instead, the basic brain architecture was simply given upgrades, with newer brain structures added to the old ones.

Deep within the brain's temporal lobe, the almond-shaped amygdala is where the action is when it comes to raw fear responses that mobilize immediate, subconscious decision-making and quick actions. But the amygdala is not subtle and it's not judicious. In an office suite, or a midtown restaurant, or the family kitchen, it can pick up signals it perceives as threatening and trigger the overwhelming fear response that we call an "amygdala hijack." This is what happened to Brad day in and day out at work. Amygdala hijack can cause people to lash out at others verbally. In more severe cases, people may become violent and assault others. For Brad, it was what brought an otherwise exemplary run at the company he'd cofounded to an unhappy end.

What Kahneman calls "system 2" thinking, on the other hand, is slow, ponderous, and deliberative. It's within system 2 that opportunities for active inquiry and Think Talk Create come alive. But system 2 requires substantial energy, effort, self-discipline, and focus—none of which is easily accessible when the brain and the bloodstream are flooded with the stress hormones and neurotransmitters of fight or flight. Active inquiry is such a remarkable achievement because system 2 processing is so energy draining, so hard to come by. When Brad was stressed out and bossing people around in the office, system 1—driven by the amygdala and other limbic structures in the emotion centers of his brain—was the predominant force. We will soon see how, with sustained effort, he went on to enhance his system 2 capacities, to the benefit of his personal and professional life.

The dynamic interplay of the limbic system, the frontal lobe, and personhood recalls some themes from ancient Greek philosophy. A counterpoint to the Phineas Gage story is the *Phaedrus*, one of the many dialogues of Plato, who presented Socrates's oral teachings to the world in written form. His discourse on love includes the famous allegory of the chariot, meant to illustrate the tripartite nature of the human soul, or psyche.[5] The Greeks were strong on philosophical idealism and weak on anatomy and physiology, but the basic storyline here is that there are two winged horses pulling this chariot, one mortal, the other immortal. The mortal one is dark and stubborn; the immortal one is white and noble and pure. At the reins is the charioteer, hoping to control these two competing beasts on an ascent to the "heaven" of everlasting truth and absolute knowledge. The white horse is ready to rise, but the dark horse keeps tugging the chariot back down toward earth.

For Plato, the dark horse was the base appetites, the white horse was "spiritedness" or the quest for honor, and the charioteer was reason. Even though the Greeks exalted reason above all else, Plato recognized that humans are not automatons, and that a life worth living depends on harnessing all our aspects and energies, despite their contradictions, and channeling them toward worthy goals. Plato saw the task primarily as getting the dark horse under control through the influence of reason, combined with some aspects of the spirited, honor-seeking white horse. The goal was to achieve "the harmony of the soul," which Plato saw as fundamental to any noble endeavor.

Today we may use different terms for the various attributes and ground them more in physical structures (most notably, the brain) than in idealized Platonic forms, but we certainly agree with Plato that intellect, emotion, and a kind of spiritual longing all need to be brought together, each leavening and modulating the excesses of the other. The expert needs to combine a keen focus on analytical details with thoughtful awareness of the emotional needs of his collaborators, all in the service of growth, profitability, and thriving (or whatever the broader vision may be). In any workplace situation, that kind of integration is the function of active inquiry and Think Talk Create. Brad hadn't learned how to do it yet, but it wasn't game over for him.

Getting Unstuck

Brad came to executive coaching for practical solutions. The coach wanted to help him implement a plan to enhance his active inquiry skills. But Brad at first reacted just as defensively and angrily to the coaching feedback as he had toward his colleagues. He was convinced that no one understood his intentions. He couldn't absorb the idea that, even if there was some imbalance in his coworkers' perceptions of him, their perceptions mattered. If they misunderstood his motives, it was his responsibility to find a new way to communicate, one that allowed them to view him as a trusted collaborator rather than as a hostile and damaging adversary. The coaching seemed to be at an early impasse. How could it get unstuck?

At the coach's prompting, Brad scanned the other parts of his life and other meaningful relationships for chances to practice new approaches to social interactions. One golden opportunity was with his teenage son, who was struggling academically and had fallen in with a crowd that Brad worried about. He feared that this social group was partying too often, abusing drugs, and neglecting their school responsibilities. Brad wasn't sure whether (and how badly) things had declined for his son, but he knew that lecturing the kid or "getting in his face" about the problems had only backfired—just as they had made things worse at work. Perhaps developing a new conversational style at home, based on active inquiry, would translate into better skills in the workplace. Brad's love for his son seemed to open his mind to a new interpersonal approach.

Brad's confidence in active inquiry increased as he noticed that he and his son were becoming closer. The two now would take walks and go out to lunch or dinner for no particular reason, simply to have some time together. Coached on how to actively listen, Brad could ask his son, in a relaxed manner, about his teachers and his friends, his interests and activities. When Brad heard something concerning from his son about the peer group, he didn't fly off the handle but calmly asked another question. As a result, he learned more in a few conversations with his son than he had known about him over all of his teenage years. Brad was beginning to feel that he was more than just a breadwinner, disciplinarian, and role model for hard work. He was now able to experience himself as a parent in a more emotionally connected and meaningful way than he had ever imagined possible. By humanizing the conversations with his son via active inquiry, Brad realized that he was having more influence than before—the goal he had sought, but had failed to achieve, through his formerly aggressive and autocratic approach.

Sure, his son was still subject to peer pressure and vulnerable to making impulsive decisions. But it was becoming apparent to Brad that his son, like himself, was slowing down a bit more to ask himself thoughtful questions about how to handle confusing and challenging social situations. Adding this step of "pause and delay" was allowing their frontal lobes—the executive brain—to have more sway.

Having experienced the transformative effect of this way of interacting, Brad now began to think of ways he could transfer his newfound active inquiry skills into the next stage of his career. The focus of the coaching sessions in the ensuing months became about how to leverage active inquiry to succeed with colleagues in a new job.

Through active inquiry, Brad also came to realize that he wanted more than just a new position, more than simple job security. He wanted to become more fully human, and to have his deepening humanity add value in all of his relationships, with family members and in the wider world. He craved more effectiveness and influence, and he had learned the hard way that brute force can never get you there, any more than technical knowledge and a nose-to-the-grindstone work ethic can. In fact, overuse and misapplication of these strengths—trained incapacity—had been his undoing.

By applying the newly cultivated skills of active inquiry, Brad found a new job that was a better match. He was less stressed, his collaborative projects were more satisfying and energizing, and he was no longer vulnerable to the founder's syndrome that had limited his perspective on how to adapt to a growing workplace. Brad hadn't just learned a slogan— he had developed an entirely new way of interacting that should serve him well for the rest of his life.

The Dehumanized Workplace

Until he went through a major reckoning, Brad was his own worst enemy, with no one to blame but himself for his job falling apart. But it's not always so easy or fair to blame these kinds of workplace problems on any particular individual. It's also important to consider the problematic characteristics of the workplace (and the broader economy) as a whole, with multiple individuals in complex roles collectively creating toxic environments. The problem of workplace dehumanization is garnering more and more attention as a public health crisis.

In 2019, the World Health Organization made a major announcement about the crisis of workplace burnout and reported that the term had been given a more focused definition in the eleventh revision of the International Classification of Diseases (ICD) system, which serves as the standard diagnostic tool for health management. Burnout is now defined in the ICD specifically as "a syndrome conceptualized as resulting from chronic workplace stress that has not been successfully managed."[6] The three core dimensions are "feelings of energy depletion or exhaustion; increased mental distance from one's job, or feelings of negativism or cynicism related to one's job; and reduced professional efficacy." With this much clearer definition, the ICD hoped to call greater attention to the mental health pandemic plaguing workers around the globe. The COVID-19 crisis has only served to make this matter more urgent.

At a time when the number of medications to treat mood disorders and related problems has soared, the suicide rate in the United States has also increased, according to multiple organizations. In one study conducted by the National Center for Health Statistics, which looked at the years 1999 to 2014, the suicide rate in the United States increased by 24 percent.[7] In another study, the National Institute of Mental Health estimated that over a slightly longer stretch, between 1999 and 2018, the suicide rate increased by a whopping 35 percent.[8] Suicide now stands as the eighth most prevalent cause of death in the United States. What is going on here?

Economists Anne Case and Angus Deaton, in their book *Deaths of Despair and the Future of Capitalism*, have delineated how workplace problems and economic despair have wrought havoc on working-class Americans to the point that their life expectancy has been steadily decreasing for years in a row, a trend not seen in the United States for over a century. Deaths of despair—which include suicides, alcoholic liver disease, and drug overdoses—have been rising in a steady and alarming fashion in recent times. Case and Deaton point out that one of the major factors in this disquieting trend toward more self-inflicted death is that fewer people nowadays have "a long-term commitment to an employer who, in turn, was once committed to them, a relationship that, for many, conferred status and was one of the foundations of a meaningful life."[9]

The negative impact of this trend has been profound. In 2019, the Republican senator from Florida, Marco Rubio, wrote a piece for *First Things*—a public journal about the intersection of religion and public life—in which he referenced a papal encyclical called *Rerum novarum*. This open letter to the church hierarchy, written in 1891 by Pope Leo XIII, addressed the need for some amelioration of "the misery and wretchedness pressing so unjustly on the majority of the working class."[10] The pope argued that work and working people have a fundamental dignity that all societies are bound to respect and serve. Concurring, Rubio—a pro-business conservative—points out that the church teaches us that work is an essential part of how we fulfill our purpose in life. "In the American tradition," Rubio notes, "private business enterprise is the main institution the public has entrusted with providing dignified work."

But private business, he goes on to say, has renounced its previous role as a mainstay of human dignity.

> When dignified work is lost or unattainable, it corrodes the human spirit. Recent years have seen the destruction of jobs that provided a way of life for families and communities for generations. Despite the claims that a "new economy" would rescue them, the new fabric of American work is not thick enough to sustain them. Entire regions have been hollowed out. Even among those who have succeeded by the terms of the financial economy, there is an inescapable sense that their work is not productive in the way it was for generations prior. The Church emphasizes the moral duty of employers to respect workers not just as means to profit, but as human persons and productive members of their community and nation. We must recover this wisdom and remember what economics is truly for.[11]

Addressing this trend with regard to physical and mental health, Stanford business professor Jeffrey Pfeffer, in his book *Dying for a Paycheck: How Modern Management Harms Employee Health and Company Performance—and What We Can Do About It*, describes how a maniacal hunger for profit

leads companies to behave in ways that are inimical to productivity, sustainability, and basic wellness.[12] Not only do
toxic work environments harm quality of life and reduce
productivity during work hours, but by extension they wreak
havoc on people's personal lives as well. Inadequate work-
life balance means strained marriages, low-quality time
with children, and less energy for basic wellness activities
like exercise, sleep, and nutrition. Psychiatric conditions and
chronic medical problems like diabetes and hypertension,
which are caused or exacerbated by stress, are the potentially
lethal results. "I didn't think the workplace would be the
fifth leading cause of death in the United States," Pfeffer
said in an interview about his research. "And, by the way,
when I talk to HR people, they say the numbers we have are
certainly wrong: They are too low."[13]

A particularly shocking example of workplace-related
deaths calls the problem into stark relief. In 2019, a French
court concluded that the former chief executive of France
Télécom (now the telecom giant Orange) along with his
second-in-command and the human resources director were
responsible for the suicides of thirty-five employees (plus
the attempted suicides of others) in the mid- to late 2000s.[14]
These French executives were criminally convicted of "institutional moral harassment" and punished with four-month
prison sentences and hefty personal fines, in addition to fines
levied against Orange.

In their attempt to get about 22,000 of the 120,000 employees off the payroll during a major corporate restructuring

necessitated by a $50 billion debt, the executives had purposely bred an atmosphere of fear and anxiety in the workplace. A *New York Times* article reported on employees' testimony about "despairing colleagues who hanged themselves, set themselves on fire, or threw themselves out of windows, under trains, and off bridges and highway overpasses as the company deliberately reassigned them to roles for which they were ill-suited, in order to reduce the workforce."[15]

The youngest suicide victim, twenty-eight-year-old Nicolas Grenoville, was a diligent, introverted technician whose job had always been to work alone—as he preferred to do—on phone lines. When he was maliciously thrust into a world of extroverts in a sales position for which he had little aptitude and no training, he simply couldn't tolerate it. "I can't stand this job anymore, and France Télécom couldn't care less," he wrote before hanging himself with an internet cable in 2009. "All they care about is money." There had never been a criminal conviction in France for what the unions representing employees like Grenoville labeled an intentional form of "social violence."

Superficial Band-Aid solutions will not stop this ongoing trend toward burnout and premature death. Many companies have made well-intentioned efforts to improve the quality of the workplace by providing meditation sessions, massage chairs, and Ping-Pong tables for employees who need a "wellness" break. Some companies are giving free access to mindfulness apps such as Headspace, which provides structured and guided meditation experiences. Many employees are given free gym memberships and wearable devices to monitor the number of steps they take each day, sometimes with rewards for hitting a goal. None of these offerings is a bad thing in itself, but these efforts can only be helpful within the context of a fundamental shift in workplace values. This can only occur via open dialogue about the long-term health of workers and the company as a whole—which is, in essence, the sum total of those individuals. In the chapters that follow, we will continue to explore this problem and how the Think Talk Create process can provide sound, sustainable solutions in the years to come.

5

THE HEARTLESSNESS
OF THE MATTER

Workplace Dehumanization
and Its Vicissitudes

For two decades Marc had worked for Primary Insurance, a small local agency located in suburban Toronto that almost exclusively served customers within a fifty-mile radius. His first twenty years there were happy ones, and he would have been delighted to spend another twenty. There was a clear sense of purpose at work: serving the community and helping the people you bumped into at parent-teacher events, neighbors standing in line at the grocery store, or even a former manager whose house had caught fire. Company picnics were a blast, the holiday parties never disappointed, and when you sat in a meeting with colleagues, even from other departments, you knew what grade their kids were in.

A Biblical Job's Toxic Job

Then Primary was acquired by FMF Life, one of the world's largest insurance companies—a big, global agency head-quartered hundreds of miles away. Both the sense of purpose and the sense of belonging to a team began to fade. Now you were lucky to know half the people on any given email chain, never mind anything about their children.

When Marc walked into his office one morning, it looked as if a hurricane had blown through overnight. He was shocked to find his favorite family portrait facedown on the floor beside his desk. As he surveyed the room, coffee cup in hand, Marc also noticed that the wind appeared to have been selective. On every desk, employee computers, mouse pads, keyboards, and telephones were still in place. The only things knocked onto the carpet were photographs and other small personal items.

Some weeks after the merger, the new team members had been sent a memo from corporate headquarters about proper office protocol. In this all-hands bulletin, manage-ment had informed Marc and his colleagues that no personal items were to be kept on desks. No calendars, no decora-tions, no photographs—only company-provided equipment necessary for work. Even though Marc's accounting depart-ment was internal, which is to say customers never entered their offices, there was to be absolutely nothing of a personal nature anywhere in sight.

The initial reaction of Marc and his colleagues was along the lines of "Can you believe this? What are they thinking?

They must have a lot of time on their hands." But of course those new to FMF Life went along and internalized the message, assuming that it meant there were to be no holiday decorations, "Hang In There" cat posters, or football calendars, but that pictures of their kids would surely be okay. Not only was corporate headquarters a long plane ride away (or, as the Chinese say, "The emperor is far away and the mountains are high"), but many of the team leaders from before the merger were still in place. Could the corporate culture really change so dramatically? Could it become that impersonal overnight?

In a word, yes.

The big wind that had blown in to dump family photos on the floor was not a hurricane, but a team of senior managers who'd flown in from FMF Life corporate on an unannounced visit in the middle of the night. With no heads-up, they'd entered the office, turned on the lights, and methodically walked from desk to desk, sweeping all personal items onto the floor like snow off a windshield. They'd then switched off the lights, locked the doors, and gone back to their hotel. Standing in the office the following morning, mouths agape, Marc and his fellow workers slowly and confusedly picked up cherished keepsakes and carefully placed them in bags to be carried home by the end of the day.

When the visiting senior managers appeared to greet their new colleagues that morning, they made no mention of their midnight raid, and they offered no apologies. Marc would soon learn that this was par for the course for his new corporate overlords. FMF Life treated their human employees the same way they treated the office furniture. The furniture was part of the "physical plant." The people were "human resources" from which to extract value, a means to an end and nothing more. It flew in the face of the core principle of the moral philosophy of Immanuel Kant: always treat another person as an end in himself, never merely as a means.

These managers weren't simply a few bad apples that spoiled the whole bunch. They embraced a professionally ingrained, "numbers only" thought process that knows no limit. It's a mindset that can touch or at least influence almost every business decision, including ones in which human beings are displaced in favor of less expensive automated processes.

The managers weren't bad people; they were ordinary people indoctrinated to act badly. One of the most familiar clichés in mobster movies is for someone to say, "Hey, it's not personal. It's just business." Social psychology research has suggested that people's unethical behavior is more likely to be tolerated in workplaces if they are high performers. A 2016 study published in the journal *Personnel Psychology*, which incorporated surveys from over one thousand people (including three hundred pairs of supervisors and their employees), concluded that supervisors and coworkers tolerate various forms of unethical behavior when productivity is strong.[1] People have learned that coldness and ruthlessness may be acceptable, even helpful, when it comes to short-term gains. If that's the case, then so much the worse for empathy and basic human dignity.

Why would a modern manager deny an employee like Marc a workplace reminder of his loved ones—and by so doing deprive him of the opportunity for what some psychologists call "social snacking" (such as a glance at a photograph), which is considered beneficial for stress reduction and mental health—when it runs against science and sound economics? These managers may have missed the recent science on dehumanization. They seem to be stuck in Milton Friedman's mindset that short-term shareholder value alone must determine business decisions.

For the Primary Insurance employees who suddenly found themselves working in a very different environment at FMF Life, the policy regarding no personal items on desks was only one of many dehumanizing new rules. Vacation time was shortened and allocated to each employee based on seniority. Employees hired within the past five years who had been promised three weeks off now saw it cut to two weeks. Marc, a veteran of more than two decades, saw his vacation cut from five to four weeks. Some employees, many of whom carried over a decade of experience but had left immediately following the merger, were informed that their seniority would be disregarded if they wished to return. Even if they had deep knowledge of institutional history, they would restart with only entry-level benefits. Along with these changes came another caveat: all employee time off was to be approved by corporate headquarters, and any employee with three unexcused absences would be terminated immediately.

In mid-September, Marc awoke one morning to find his wife severely ill and needing to go to the emergency room. Before the merger, this would have meant a quick phone call to his boss explaining the circumstances, but it now required an extensive email exchange to detail the reason for the absence. Having already submitted his request for time off during the holidays, Marc had zero days remaining, even if it was due to a family emergency. For the sake of his wife's health, Marc was forced to take an unexcused absence. Strike one.

Not long after his wife's recovery, a surprise early winter storm began to form in the middle of October. Meteorologists predicted considerable snow and ice accumulation over a three-day period, making the morning commute virtually impossible. State and local officials held a press conference to declare a state of emergency. For their safety, all motorists were advised to keep off the roads. FMF Life's policy, though, was for the insurance agency to remain open 24/7/365. It never closed on weekends. Phone lines remained open in the middle of the night, even on holidays, when a skeleton crew manned the ship. Unsure how corporate headquarters would react to a life-threatening blizzard, Marc and his colleagues quietly wondered what they should do. Their questions were answered at 3 p.m., when an email arrived from the home office.

Given the state of emergency, and because "we at corporate headquarters care greatly about your safety," team members should "use their best judgment" as to whether or not they were able to drive to work safely on the snow-filled roads. But all employees were expected to report to work. Anticipating that the drive might be unsafe, the agency had hired drivers with large SUVs to act as taxis for those unwilling to brave the roads and attempt the commute alone. Making his way out to the driveway the following morning, snow shovel in hand, Marc was greeted by another surprise from Mother Nature: a snapped tree lay on top of his car. Before calling even his own insurance agent, Marc dropped his shovel and hurriedly dialed the number for the SUV service. Pickups were already underway on the carefully mapped route. No driver would be able to reach Marc until later that morning, possibly not even until lunchtime. Overcome with a profound sense of defeat, Marc made his way back inside and begrudgingly logged on to the attendance platform. As snow continued to pile up on the windowsill, he clicked "submit" for his second unexcused absence. Strike two.

Never once that summer had Marc anticipated being one unexcused absence away from losing the job where he'd been a highly productive contributor for nearly twenty years. During his entire tenure with the small agency, such an idea would have seemed preposterous. He'd always felt valued and respected, that his contributions mattered. That was before his company went global and replaced human values with the shareholder-driven numbers game.

Toward the end of the summer, when staff received the vacation and attendance directive, Marc had made a quick calculation. With the vacation days he had left for the year, he could still visit his relatives during the winter holidays. But there was another important event, scheduled for a Friday in December, that was far more important. Marc's daughter would be getting married and he would be escorting her down the aisle. A few days after the storm, Marc scheduled a phone meeting with the senior manager in charge of personnel. He explained the incredible circumstances. A medical emergency and a natural disaster, both of which were well beyond his control, had forced him to miss two days of work. And now his daughter's wedding was less than two months away.

Marc's plea was simple: Could the agency allow him to miss a third, unexcused day of work without losing his job? Management's answer was equally simple: no. The policy of the agency had been made clear following the merger, the numbers were the numbers, and no employee would receive special treatment. Then, in what can best be described as a rhetorical cri de coeur, Marc asked, "So I have to choose between attending my daughter's wedding and losing my job?" "Everyone is replaceable," said the voice on the other end of the line. Then all Marc heard was the dial tone buzzing in his ear.

Overburdened and Undervalued

Research over the past five decades has shown what can happen when people like Marc are denied autonomy, when they are betrayed, humiliated, socially excluded, or not recognized as human. The Whitehall study, conducted in Britain in the mid-twentieth century, examined mortality rates among civil servants, based on rank, for those between the ages of thirty-five and fifty-five. The results are just as alarming today as when they were first published. Civil servants at the bottom of the pyramid were three times more likely to die at a young age than those sitting at the top. The researchers found a direct causal relationship between fatal events, such as heart attack or stroke, and the stresses placed upon those forced to carry the workload without a sense of control or any feeling that their contribution mattered. That's not to say people at the top don't face stress—they do—but it's interesting to note that those forced to lift the hammer, so to speak, are more prone to an earlier death than those giving the commands.

According to University of British Columbia psychologist Kalina Christoff, careful analysis reveals that dehumanizing professional environments "directly contribute to depression, anxiety, and stress-related disorders."[2] A 2018 study found that workplace stress was strongly correlated with moderate to severe suicidal ideation.[3] This finding was preceded by the 2015 study in the *American Journal of Preventive Medicine* (noted in the Introduction) that concluded that one of the primary factors for the tragic spike in suicides was "distress about jobs."[4] More and more workers are overburdened and undervalued. These are people, not rubber bands. Both can wear down and snap, but with far different consequences.

While suicide is an extreme event, and relatively rare, the risk to overall health posed by working for a dehumanized organization is a chronic and pervasive problem. Thanks to a convergence of research from the medical, neurological, and business fields, there is a growing body of evidence that severely bottom-line-oriented companies—those that subscribe to the concept of maximizing shareholder value to such a degree that it sacrifices the well-being of employees—are indirectly (or directly) responsible for the untimely deaths of employees. Trying to reach sales goals is one thing, but dying to do so is another.

The research follows three key points: First, according to the World Economic Forum, an enormous percentage of the health-care burden in the developed world, roughly 75 percent, comes from chronic disease—illnesses such as diabetes and cardiovascular or circulatory disease. Second, there is an overwhelming amount of medical literature that suggests these illnesses—and the unhealthy behaviors they coincide with, such as overeating, underexercising, and drug and alcohol abuse—stem from mental health problems like depression, anxiety, and stress-related disorders. Third, as we already know full well, an equally large set of data shows that work can be one, if not the greatest, source of depression, anxiety, and stress-related disorders if people feel squeezed.[5]

This phenomenon whereby employees die because of unrelenting quantitative pressure is hardly new. In Japan, employee mortality rates for young staff reached such staggering levels over the previous few decades that it was given a name: *karōshi*, which translates to "overwork death." The government and other organizations, including regional businesses, implemented concrete programs to curb the fatalities. Overtime limits were capped, a hotline was developed, and high-risk employees were required to speak with a mental health professional. Some other countries have not yet caught up.

Marc thought about what his wife's reaction would be when he told her he lost his job, or his daughter's when he told her he'd only be able to attend the evening reception at her wedding. Marc and his wife still had a mortgage, college loan payments, and—thanks to the storm—one fewer car. From a financial perspective, losing his job was just not an option. His daughter understandably showed greater empathy than company management. He would be at the wedding, she told him, even if it meant they had to change the date. And change the date they did. Marc's daughter, after considerable negotiation with caterers and venue managers and then getting word out to all the guests, shifted the event forward from Friday to Saturday so her father could avoid the third strike that would cost him his job.

But Marc had had enough. As the year came to a close, he counted down the days until his winter vacation, hoping the change of scenery would buoy his spirits. He was frequently sad, worried, and, most of all, tired. During the flight home from their vacation on New Year's Day, while Marc anxiously tapped his fingers in anticipation of work the following morning, his wife suggested that it was time to make a change. His job was taking too great a toll. This new year would be Marc's twenty-fourth at the company. At

Primary Insurance, those who reached the twenty-five-year mark were generously entitled to additional retirement benefits. Though FMF Life certainly had no similar program in place for its own employees, it had been agreed that new team members absorbed from Primary would not lose this privilege.

Well aware of the benefit program, and having considered their financial future, Marc made a deal with his wife. It was one year, he told her. He could endure twelve more months. He would cut back on vacation, save two full weeks for unforeseen occurrences, and meet with a therapist every month to talk through the emotions he was feeling. Once the year was over and Marc received his incentives, he would retire from the agency and find other work he was more passionate about. She agreed. On January 2, Marc walked through the doors, sat at his pictureless desk, and quietly murmured to himself: "I can do this."

Marc kept his word. As the months passed, he incurred no unexcused absences. But the only source of joy he and his colleagues found in their workday was the box of tissues on each of their desks. Though personal items had been eliminated, employees had been allowed to keep a box of tissues handy, which they were asked to purchase out of pocket. As a show of individualism and personal expression, they began to use the tissue boxes as subversive decorations. Some were vibrantly colored, others showed a favorite sports team, but they all stood out. And with every outlandish new tissue box that arrived at the office, employees winked at one another in solidarity, acknowledging their subtle rebellion.

Finally, the year came to a close, and since his holiday travel had been postponed, Marc found himself in the office on the morning of December 1, twenty-four years and 364 days since he'd first walked into the small, local insurance agency as a wide-eyed newcomer. During the previous twelve months he had hung tough and accomplished what he set out to do. Marc's boss greeted him at his desk that morning and told him that a representative from company headquarters wanted to speak with him in a nearby conference room. Marc walked down the hall and into a room where he saw a stranger sitting at the table. The stranger's suit and tie seemed to blend with the sterile wallpaper behind him, as if he were wearing a recently developed form of office camouflage. The meeting didn't last long.

Company leadership had been evaluating a number of options to cut costs. The agency's expenses had risen over the previous two quarters and shareholders were starting to get nervous. In an effort to "trim the fat," the CEO had suggested a review of employees whose time at the firm entitled them to higher pay and increased benefits but whose job could be performed by a less experienced, less costly member of the team. As a result, Marc's position was being eliminated and his services were no longer required—one day shy of his twenty-fifth anniversary. At that moment, a security guard entered the room with a small box. Inside was Marc's bag, coffee mug, some pens and pencils from home, and the box of tissues that had sat atop his desk. He was asked to leave the building and would be escorted to the front door by the security guard. As he made his way toward the exit, Marc saw only the flickers of vibrantly colored tissue boxes across a sea of gray desks and cubicle walls, a final sparkle of humanity in an otherwise monochromatic and lifeless place of business.

Companies like FMF Life are at risk of falling into the same trap as the brilliant Dr. Fisher and the well-meaning clinicians who treated Ramon: adherence to oversimplified data that can blind us to the most essential human truths. And yet, as we saw in the Introduction, human dignity, health, and fair compensation are not incompatible with institutional growth and professional success. In fact, they're essential over the long haul. Findings backed by cognitive science and organizational research note that reinvigorating the workplace with a sense of humanity dramatically increases the chances of success. After all, recent studies suggest that upward of 80 percent of the workday is spent engaging in collaborative activity, a 50 percent increase over the past twenty years.[6]

McKinsey recently published a report that confirmed what Google had discovered through Project Aristotle. "The hardest activities to automate with currently available technologies are those that involve managing and developing people or that apply expertise to decision making, planning, or creative work."[7] The irony, then, is that as so much of the rote work of business is transferred to algorithms, the most valuable work for humans to perform will require being, in a sense, more human.

Of course, degrading, abusive workplaces are hardly unique to modern life. Paid laborers—children, women, people of color, immigrants, and low-skilled men—have been devalued and mistreated throughout history, with no explanation from their employer other than "Because we can." In another sad irony, it took labor shortages created by the Black Death to see any improvement in the treatment of serfs in medieval Europe. Today, the novel coronavirus seems to have reminded us that the workers who are truly essential are often the lowest paid. There's nothing like a deadly virus to make us appreciate the minimum-wage worker, often a recent immigrant, who comes in at night to sanitize the bathroom. In a time of face masks and extreme social isolation, we might also come to better appreciate the intangible and unquantifiable benefits of a warm smile and human touch.

Goodbye to Hello

At the age of ninety-two, Marge was one of Walmart's most loyal customers. She lived alone in the modest house her parents purchased after World War II, on a quiet residential street in a small New England city. Apart from occasional interactions with her neighbors when getting the mail or taking out her trash, she had only intermittent visits from distant relatives who came to check in on her. Lonely, though, she was not—for Marge lived less than five minutes away from her local Walmart.

Every morning after breakfast, Marge drove the short distance to the megastore. When she entered, she'd often hear a happy employee loudly announce, "Here she is, the queen of Walmart!" Walmart provided Marge with a sense of community. And it all started with greeters who intuitively used active inquiry in their open-ended questions, which might at first glance appear artificial: "How are you this morning?" or "How's it going today?" These questions are intended to help shoppers feel welcome. But for Marge—who went there day after day, year after year—genuine relationships had formed as a result of these earnest inquiries. The seemingly boiler-plate questions actually were genuine invitations to conversation. Marge wasn't expected simply to say a superficial "Fine, how are you?" in response. Over time, she and many of the greeters truly got to know and grew to care about each other, in much the same way the custodians and assisted-living residents described in Chapter 2 had done.

Having a sense that Walmart was her place, Marge was encouraged to return over and over again. And what happened when she returned? She spent money. The low-wage greeters, in their unalloyed humanity and kindness, had unwittingly developed yet another paying customer for the nation's largest corporation.

Walmart gave Marge a sense of belonging, and the greeter's face was the first one she saw every morning. What she didn't know was that the greeters would soon be out of a job, or at best reassigned. Back in 2016, the company began reshaping the roles and responsibilities of greeters, many of whom had physical and mental disabilities. Walmart's intentions were to replace greeters with "customer hosts." According to company mandate, "to qualify for these new host positions, workers must be able to lift 25 pounds, clean up spills, collect carts, and stand for long periods of time," each of which can pose a challenge for those with varying physical, speech, or cognitive impairments.[8] Many greeters understandably felt targeted by this new policy and fearful that they'd lose their beloved jobs.

Walmart claimed to have made the shift to "offer more to customers at the door," though the company acknowledged the new policy could adversely affect disabled workers. As one reporter noted, "Retailers are under a lot of pressure to keep down costs, and Walmart in particular has been jockeying for dominance against one of its biggest rivals, Amazon."[9] Back in 2005, an internal company memo had been leaked that questioned whether all jobs should require the ability to perform physical activity, presumably to ensure the hiring of a healthy workforce and thereby cut rising healthcare costs. Was health insurance for workers with disabilities too heavy a burden?

Walmart already had questionable pay-scale policies. The average hourly pay of a standard Walmart associate is $14.26.[10] Meanwhile, in 2018, Walmart's CEO was paid $24 million in annual compensation, which amounts to

$11,538 per hour—more than seven hundred times as much as those lowest on the pay scale.[11] To us as outsiders, it certainly appears that the company's margins could allow for a more humane attitude toward its least fortunate employees. Not only does Walmart sit atop the Fortune 500, but it's also the United States' largest private employer, with a staggering 1.5 million workers scattered throughout its headquarters, distribution centers, and big-box stores. In 2019, the company posted annual revenue of roughly $515 billion.[12]

Termination of the greeter program was a loss for Marge, for the community, and for the disabled individuals who had found meaning and purpose in their work. How much had the company really saved as a result of killing this program? It's hard to see how any cost savings would have justified the loss of morale for workers, the reputation damage to the company (which suffered badly in the press for its poor treatment of the greeters), and the moral self-degradation of the company's willingness to sacrifice hardworking employees with disabilities to possibly gain a fraction of a percentage point on the bottom line. Ironically, Walmart may even have lost on the deal. It is conceivable that their balance sheet suffered just a bit, as previously loyal customers like Marge chose to start shopping in more hospitable retail outlets.

Some companies today make the mistake of assuming that the numbers are all that matter, to the point that any objection to this line of thinking is met with the notion that "it's just how business works." But, as evidenced from Marc's traumatic firing and Marge's loss of her community connections, this mindset can result in senseless and needless cruelty. Would Walmart's profitability really have shrunk at all if it had maintained or even expanded the greeter program? What did treating Marc like a broken stapler really do for FMF Life? This approach to doing business arises directly out of the suspect belief that increasing shareholder value is the only true barometer of business success. We will now turn our attention to this insidious problem and how it continues to threaten the vitality of contemporary workplaces and society more broadly.

6

UNSAFETY IN NUMBERS

When Shareholder Value
Is All That Matters

W hy do corporations feel the need to be so hard-hearted? More than that, why do they feel so justified in this stance? Why do perfectly decent people, who may be pillars of their communities, loving to their families, and exemplars of charitable giving, come to their offices and behave like the robber barons of old?

Well, along with the ebb and flow of political trends in the last hundred years—regulation and reform, followed by deregulation and the return of laissez-faire attitudes—a conceptual revolution took place beginning in the 1970s that, in some circles, gave intellectual respectability to behaviors that fly in the face of basic sanity and any respectable code of ethics. This conceptual revolution is far from over; we are still in its grip and confronting an epic societal struggle to coalesce around a higher set of shared values. Before we describe today's crisis in detail, we'll present some of the antecedents to the enshrining of shareholder value as the one and only measure of business success.

Body Count

For years, there's been a growing awareness of the problem of sweatshops in the developing world, where adults and children perform mind-numbing, often dangerous tasks in awful conditions for pitiful wages. But in the American heartland as well, workers in such places as meatpacking plants and Amazon logistics centers face conditions that harken back to the era of Upton Sinclair and *The Jungle*.

COVID-19 made the dangers of these conditions far more severe: as workers faced a "your job or your life" dilemma, many employers doubled down, demanding compliance. Amazon, for example, provided much-needed jobs during the economic shutdown, but in April 2020 the company also fired many workers who spoke out in the name of safety—even though corporate profits were soaring. Amazon in each case cited justifiable reasons for the firings. Regardless, the company's drive for never-ending revenue growth seemed, at least to public perception, to outstrip the value of protecting the health of workers and preventing community spread of COVID-19.

The only upside is that the extreme situation of the pandemic reawakened awareness of long-standing inhumane work conditions driven merely by corporate greed, as well as people's simple need for a job in a tight economy with inadequate safety nets. We could trace the history of such exploitation through millennia, but the classic American story of the unsafe workplace dates back to the beginning of the twentieth century, when it was common practice for factory workers in Manhattan to arrive at 7 a.m., "enjoy" a thirty-minute lunch break, and not go home until 8 p.m. or later. The work was Sunday through Saturday and the wage was less than a dollar per day. Air quality and sanitation were so bad that government staffers investigating mistreatment of the predominantly immigrant workforce occasionally became ill themselves. One reformer recalled seeing "whole families, mothers with their children, little boys and girls, working all the daylight hours seven days a week in rooms in which there was not a single window."[1]

On one inspection, state officials investigated a factory where the owner was accused of employing workers under the age of seven. Flatly denying the accusation, factory managers ushered the investigators through the production area to demonstrate that everything was as it should be and that they were adhering to a high standard of ethics. Satisfied with their observations, the investigators were preparing to leave when a state official accidentally pushed the wrong elevator call button. When the doors opened, they found several young children, well under the age of seven, crammed into the tiny compartment. Management had packed the children into the elevator and moved them to another floor in an effort to conceal the company's exploitation of children.

But even these too-little-too-late inspections never would have taken place without the tragedy in March 1911 at the Triangle Shirtwaist Factory, which at the time occupied the eighth, ninth, and tenth floors of a building that still overlooks Washington Square Park.

The shirtwaist was a comfortable blouse that had become very popular and been made affordable by advances in mass-production techniques, which did not require skilled workers. Impoverished immigrants were arriving at Ellis Island on a daily basis, ready to enter the factories in their quest for the American dream.

Back in 1911, the Triangle Shirtwaist Factory lacked lavatory facilities, so employees had to leave the building to access the nearest bathroom. Dissatisfied with this interruption of work, factory management began locking the steel exit doors to ensure that production did not suffer. Only the factory foreman had the key.

On Saturday, March 25, an employee working on the tenth floor lit a cigarette, waved the match to extinguish the flame, and tossed it alongside other debris scattered about the workspace. But the match was not fully extinguished. In less than a minute, the room was engulfed in flames. Terrified, the workers rushed to the exits, only to find them locked. Locating the foreman and asking him to unlock all of the doors on three factory levels was simply impossible. The dry wood, fabric, and scraps that covered the area ignited like gasoline.

Some workers were crushed to death by the sheer force of five hundred people pushing frantically to dislodge the heavy steel barricades that trapped them inside. Others suffocated as the heat and smoke consumed what little toxic air remained. In a desperate effort for survival, some smashed windows, which only fueled the blaze. Those screaming for help through shards of broken glass had little time to decide whether to jump or risk burning to death. "Bodies smashed against the sidewalks and tore through sidewalk gratings" as horrified onlookers watched nearly sixty women, some as young as fifteen, plummet to their deaths.[2] In the twenty-minute span between the match hitting the floor and the fire department gaining control over the blaze, 146 workers perished while hundreds more were severely burned. The story epitomizes an attitude toward workers that, despite more regulatory protections now, persists. More than 350,000 people attended the joint funeral for the Triangle employees. But what those 350,000 people didn't know was that the deaths were the result of the company's owners seeing bathroom breaks as an unacceptable interruption of factory output.

One tragedy after another brought certain grudging reforms during the Progressive Era, but the First World War interrupted progress, and in the postwar boom known as the Roaring Twenties, President Calvin Coolidge declared that "the business of America is business." So it wasn't until the ensuing stock market crash, Great Depression, and Second World War that federal regulations, the growth of unions, and, most of all, a sense that we're all in this together truly reshaped the workplace.

Countless reforms to ensure humane working conditions followed in the decades after the Triangle Shirtwaist Factory fire in an effort to prevent such a tragedy from repeating itself. Worker safety and well-being was regarded more highly than ever before, and the leaders of many organizations adopted an attitude of responsibility. The labor movement in the United States brought reforms and improvements, but the classic corporate mindset had only gone underground, transforming itself in ways that may be less obviously dramatic than in 1911. In 2018, for example, Amazon announced that it was raising its minimum hourly wage to $15 per hour but also ceasing its practice of giving company stock to thousands of lower-level employees. As reported in the *New York Times*, the move by Amazon "will prevent employees from directly partaking in one of the greatest examples of wealth creation," the ability to own and profit from company stock.[3]

Out of post–World War II prosperity and industrial expansion came the new, quantitative managers, known as "whiz kids," epitomized by Robert McNamara, the president of Ford who went on to become secretary of defense under John F. Kennedy and Lyndon B. Johnson. This was the era of US escalation in Vietnam, where McNamara introduced systems analysis to public policy. As US engagement increased, progress eluded us, which was only natural because, aside from vague notions of thwarting the spread of communism, our objectives were as murky as the jungles in which young men were forced to die. Thus, the introduction of the body count as a numeric way of measuring progress. The more enemy bodies that piled up, it was argued, the stronger the conviction that we were turning the tide toward victory (this could be characterized as evidence-based warfare).

This led to the absurd tactic of "search and destroy" missions, sending soldiers and marines out to wander in the jungle for no purpose other than to engage the enemy and thus add more bodies to the tally. The tens of thousands of meaningless deaths fueled the domestic opposition to the war that brought down the Johnson presidency and tore the country apart. But quantitative analysis was just getting going. The last days of the Vietnam War saw the first hints of the revolution in personal computing that would put the spreadsheet into the hands of MBAs, turning them into quant jocks and completely transforming the nature of work.

The 1970s saw a slow but steady turning away from the anti-war, "peace and love," communal spirit of the sixties. The kids had had their say, and now it was time for the grown-ups to reclaim the mantle of authority. Watergate, the oil crisis, international terrorism, the fiscal collapse of New York City and other municipalities, and rising inflation were also unsettling. Unapologetic, quantitative selfishness gained surprising appeal. Bright young people were flocking to business schools, and corporate America was all in. By the end of the decade, ballot propositions were putting caps on local taxes, which "required" cuts in social services, including assistance for mental health problems.

Then came Ronald Reagan, union busting, rollbacks in federal regulations, and the advent of the yuppie, epitomized by a "He Who Dies with the Most Toys Wins" bumper sticker on a BMW. By the end of the next decade, the most lauded public figures were not great scientists, artists, or humanitarians but "masters of the universe" on Wall Street. Gordon Gekko, a fictionalized version of corporate raider Ivan Boesky, summed up the age with his infamous quote, "Greed is good."

But greed isn't good. And just as in 1911, greed can kill.

Return on Investment

The conceptual groundwork for this way of doing business was laid by the famed economist Milton Friedman at the University of Chicago. A pioneer in applied mathematical economics, Friedman wrote a rather transparent article in 1970, aptly titled "The Social Responsibility of Business Is to Increase Its Profits." In the piece, he assigned individuals in the workplace to one of two roles: principal or agent. In a corporation, the principal is the owner of the business and the CEO is an agent. It's the responsibility of the CEO, Friedman argued, to act as an agent solely in accordance with the wishes of the principal. The duty of the agent is, therefore, to "make as much money as possible while conforming to their basic rules of the society." The duty is so strict that any businessperson speaking of a "social conscience" would essentially be espousing "pure and unadulterated socialism."[4] (The CEO also could be sued by activist investors if he or she failed to "maximize shareholder value.")

"There is one and only one social responsibility of business," Friedman wrote. "To use its resources and engage in activities designed to increase its profits so long as it stays within the rules of the game."[5] This was Calvin Coolidge all over again, this time with a mathematical underpinning and a dose of Ayn Rand.

Friedman's endorsement of a return to a more Darwinian capitalism began to spread in economics departments, especially at business schools. As Friedman-influenced MBA students reached the higher rungs of the corporate ladder, companies adopted Friedman's thinking almost universally.

Michael Jensen, a professor at Harvard Business School, wrote a seminal article that codified Friedman's ideas. Additionally, it not only argued in favor of narrowly quantitative thinking in business, but made it irresistibly attractive (and obligatory) for senior executives. The title of this 1990 article was "CEO Incentives—It's Not How Much You Pay, but How." Many shareholders, spurned by corporate raiders and takeover artists, had been feeling aggrieved and sought redress for these perceived wrongs. Building on Friedman's belief that the singular goal of any business should be making company owners as wealthy as possible, Jensen argued that paying CEOs a stable wage did nothing to incentivize their performance. If the CEOs "were being paid like bu-reaucrats," then they would "act like bureaucrats." Using quantitative models, he contended that company leadership needed to financially align itself with company ownership so that both shared mutual interests. He sought to transform bureaucratic CEOs into "value-maximizing entrepreneurs" who were to be paid with "significant amounts of company stock" instead of fixed salaries. That way, if the shareholders succeeded, the CEO succeeded.[6]

Between 1978 and 2018, during a time when the typical worker's compensation only rose by 12 percent, CEO compensation rose by a whopping 940 percent.[7] Economic inequality skyrocketed. The sense of common purpose that had brought the United States through World War II and led to the most astounding level of prosperity in our history was being dismantled, replaced by gated communities, Net-Jets, and the demise of a strong middle class.

Even some investors and investment watchdogs argued that managers were working the incentives game a little too hard. In June 2020, defense contractor Raytheon Technologies came under criticism when it tweaked the compensation package of their CEO, Gregory J. Hayes, to give him an estimated gain of $12.5 million.[8] This at a time when Raytheon had cut salaries by 10 percent and furloughed thousands of workers. One month later, McDonald's sued its former CEO Steve Easterbrook to claw back part or all of a severance package estimated to be worth more than $40 million.[9] This is the largest such dispute since Disney shareholders sued to reclaim the $140 million severance given to ousted CEO Michael Ovitz after he'd been in the job for only fourteen months.[10]

But with Friedman's ideas dancing in their heads, and their own short-term incentives clear, many CEOs still embrace the mindset that feathering their own nest is, in fact, virtuous. Many boards, made up of similarly well-compensated executives, support them in a self-serving cycle of stupendous inequity, passing along the costs in the form of higher prices for consumers. Worse, as return on investment became the sole indicator of company performance, many leaders began to apply quantitative techniques to solving human challenges in every aspect of business. In far too many places, workers not only paid the freight for their bosses' opulent lifestyles, but their jobs became a soulless, mind-numbing numbers game.

Oddly enough, the Friedman and Jensen school of thought gained support from the moral philosophy of Harvard's John Rawls, who argued that rational analysis is key to the smooth functioning of society. In his 1971 book *A Theory of Justice*, Rawls wrote that all moral decision-making should eliminate irrational feelings and replace them with strict rational analysis about fairness. According to Rawls, people must place themselves behind a "veil of ignorance," in which they exclude anything personal or emotional, in order to make decisions that promote the social contract.[11] But this Spock-like emotional numbness has obvious problems, especially if you consider that your only obligation to society is to make the most money for your investors.

Yes, if your objective is to solve the Rubik's Cube, distancing yourself from feelings and setting aside any frustration you might experience with the device can be advantageous. Emotional equanimity can put you in a clear, strategic mindset that allows you to shut out the world and focus on solving the challenge. The same is true when you're trying to hold serve in tennis or do open-heart surgery—better to be in a calm, relaxed frame of mind.

But applying that hyperrational emotional distancing when collaborating with others, or when trying to inspire others to optimal performance, contradicts everything we know from behavioral economics, social psychology, evolutionary biology, and common sense.

Writing in *Frontiers in Human Neuroscience*, psychologist Kalina Christoff summarized the growing evidence of just how wrong the Freidman-Jensen-Rawls approach is when applied to human interactions. Studies show that subtle or overt dehumanization can lead to a clear breakdown in people's thinking. "When people are mechanistically dehumanized by being treated as objects, as means to an end, or as lacking the capacity for feeling," she explains, "they tend to enter into 'cognitive deconstructive' states that are characterized by reduced clarity of thought, emotional numbing, cognitive inflexibility, and an absence of meaningful thought."[12] None of that sounds good, even in sterile office environments. Christoff rejects the view of lack of feeling as a virtue and extols the benefits of treating each other with basic respect and dignity. "Empathy is not only compatible with problem solving," she writes. "It is a crucial component of reasoning about other people's mental states."[13] Again, for anyone who values evidence-based thinking, having information about what our colleagues (and customers) are thinking and feeling is a vital component of effective analysis and team leadership.

The mindless, dehumanizing, overly quantitative professional attitude was always just one possible way for business to be conducted. We see through historical evidence that some companies have chosen to be bad actors, but there is little evidence that this is the right way to do business. It's one of many ways and, according to cognitive research, not a very good way. It gained misguided economic validation toward the latter half of the twentieth century in the work of Milton Friedman. Now, in the twenty-first century, corporations are grappling with the bedeviling challenge of adopting a new business model, one rooted in a more enlightened form of capitalism.

Safe Delivery

FedEx, a multibillion-dollar company and the world's largest airfreight firm, maintains its corporate headquarters in Memphis, Tennessee. It uses the airport just outside the city center as its "World Hub" logistics center and the base for a large proportion of its domestic and international flights. The World Hub is served by nearly two hundred flights each day and can handle over 1.5 million packages every night.[14] The company, which employs over four hundred thousand people worldwide, has brought stable and well-paying jobs to the Memphis area, where it employs over thirty thousand (including eleven thousand at the airport). In 2018, FedEx invested a billion dollars to upgrade its World Hub to support its vast and ever-expanding network.[15] The company ensured that Memphis will likely remain the most significant airfreight port in the United States for decades to come. FedEx has been a boon to the community with all the jobs and economic stabilization it has brought to the region.

FedEx's annual revenues have exceeded $60 billion for many years. In a show of its local dominance back in 2004, it purchased for $92 million the naming rights to the eighteen-thousand-seat downtown arena (FedEx Forum), where the Memphis Grizzlies of the NBA play their home games and star performers headline major concerts. FedEx is a proud hometown company, by far the largest employer in Memphis and one of just three members of the Fortune 500 headquartered there (the others being International Paper and AutoZone). Along with its gargantuan airfreight counterparts (UPS and DHL), FedEx has revolutionized the way people and corporations communicate and ship goods. It has been a premier contributor to positive growth of the global village. It was named one of *Fortune* magazine's best employers in 2018.

But even the best companies need a methodology like Think Talk Create to continue improving. FedEx's sophisticated, high-tech machinery has provided an astonishingly high level of efficiency and workplace safety. But the volume and sprawl of its operations inevitably bring dangers. Some accidents will happen when so many flights and so much machinery are utilized nonstop. Like virtually all modern-day corporations, FedEx faces the ongoing challenge of how to balance the exigencies of worker safety and profitability.

Over the last several years, some FedEx employees at the airport hub have died in work-related accidents. The US Occupational Safety and Health Administration (OSHA) has investigated and fined FedEx multiple times during this period for noncompliance with workplace safety regulations.[16] In 2015, for example, a cargo tug operator was crushed by a loaded dolly he was towing. The Tennessee state agency that is responsible for overseeing occupational safety, TOSHA, investigated the incident and concluded that FedEx "did not ensure the tug operator properly fastened the seat belt around his waist while operating the tug."[17] The agency deemed it a serious violation of government safety regulations requiring companies to protect employees against dangers and lethal hazards on the job.

Then, in late 2017, a FedEx worker was found dead under a motorized mobile conveyor-belt system.[18] She had been dragged eighty feet before anyone realized there was a problem. Her family filed a $3 million lawsuit against FedEx in 2018.[19] She was killed by the very same kind of machinery that had caused the death of another FedEx worker a few years earlier.

No facility of this type can ever guarantee safety for every worker, but the rising number of deaths in recent years at FedEx raised some eyebrows. It may be difficult or impossible to prove in a court of law that the deaths were a direct result of FedEx's drive to process more and more packages efficiently and at low cost, but it certainly is fair to inquire generally into how corporate profit motives can be balanced against worker safety following a string of workplace deaths. FedEx has the financial capacity to purchase the safest equipment available, train its workers on how to operate it appropriately, and ensure that employees are rested and alert when performing their job functions.

One of the many benefits of adopting the Think Talk Create model within a workplace is that it provides a space for employees to raise valid safety concerns and, in turn, trust that those concerns will be heard. It's an ongoing challenge for companies like FedEx, who are often doing their best to explore new strategies for success while keeping employees safe.

FedEx has, at times, struggled with cautionary messages or allegations from its own employees with respect to major safety considerations, just as many other companies do as well. For example, beside the safety of the World Hub facility stands the safety of FedEx's airplanes. Concerns have been raised that some FedEx managers retaliated against employees who came forward with safety concerns and violations of the regulatory standards set by the US Federal Aviation Administration (FAA). A major whistleblower case of this kind came to light in November 2018. "One former and two current employees at FedEx's LAX location," NBC News Los Angeles reported, "were collectively awarded millions of dollars after a jury found they were wrongfully disciplined by the courier giant after coming forward to report their allegations that the company put profits ahead of safety by not maintaining its aircraft consistent with FAA safety requirements."[20] FedEx's unfortunate actions in this case serve as an indicator of what can happen when an organization fails to place a strong emphasis on psychological safety, precluding workers from expressing their ideas and concerns openly. FedEx paid a hefty financial and reputational cost for its missteps.

FedEx has touted its upgraded World Hub and other innovations as an advance in worker safety. But financial exigencies stemming from fiduciary obligations to shareholders are likely to continue, and they warrant close monitoring by regulators like OSHA and the FAA. Ideally, FedEx will also vigorously regulate itself and continue to invest in a safe, humane workplace as a top priority going forward. In light of recent deaths of employees, company executives will hopefully engage in robust active inquiry and Think Talk Create. They will have to non-defensively ask themselves and colleagues what the company can do to prevent this kind of negative publicity, avoid lawsuits and fines, attract and retain a strong workforce, and—perhaps most importantly—present itself as a good corporate citizen, a profitable giant that treats people with dignity and strives to do the right thing.

Even apart from worker safety, FedEx has engaged in other business practices that are worth scrutiny and discussion, and demonstrate the value that Think Talk Create can bring to the proverbial table. For many years, FedEx paid its drivers as contractors, not employees. That practice allowed them to avoid paying them for health insurance and other benefits usually afforded to full-fledged employees (such as overtime pay, retirement accounts, and unemployment insurance). The company in 2014 came under fire for this policy, which contrasted sharply with UPS's long-standing policy of granting its drivers full employment status and access to benefits. FedEx Ground, the division of the company that delivers small packages to homes and businesses, had over thirty thousand workers whom they classified as contractors until lawsuits against the company forced change.

Those lawsuits, initiated both by drivers and by states' attorneys general, brought the practice to an end.[21] That was a positive step, but it didn't necessarily result in better conditions for workers. FedEx then outsourced some jobs to external companies, which themselves could treat the drivers as contractors.[22] The savings to FedEx and other companies that utilize similar tactics can come at a high human cost and threaten to undermine their reputation as desirable employers. A $60 billion company might ask itself whether it's worth it to not provide workers with a full benefit package.

How good can that be for business in the long term? Whether at FedEx or anywhere else in the corporate world, that's an issue that is ripe for active inquiry.

There are other examples of the challenges at FedEx as well. On a frigid night in late January 2018, a FedEx driver in East Moline, Illinois, died outside a FedEx Freight distribution center.[23] A polar vortex had come to the region, with historically low temperatures of thirty-three degrees below zero compounded by gusting winds. No one should have been outside at the time. The US Postal Service had canceled deliveries in the region on January 30 and 31; workers stayed inside to sort mail to be delivered after the weather conditions became less unforgiving. In East Moline, however, a sixty-nine-year-old FedEx worker for some reason was outside doing his job in dangerous conditions. The coroner later determined that he had died of a traumatic head injury caused by a fall. He lay dead for hours on the ground between two semitrailers right outside the distribution center. The FedEx Freight driver's death raised questions as to why he was at work at all during the deadly polar vortex. The distribution center was closed, and yet a worker died on-site.

Surely any work performed by a FedEx driver that night in East Moline was not worth it. The tragic scenario presents an obvious opportunity for active inquiry. How can FedEx, or any complex company that must address workplace safety, take the steps needed to protect its workers while also ensuring strong earnings? That key open-ended question can be addressed through the process of Think

Talk Create. Companies can adopt policies that encourage (even require) that workers regularly slow down and engage in self-reflection about how to manage on-the-job dangers. Mandatory breaks during the course of a workday, no matter how busy and intense, might help. Frequent conversations, framed by the tenets of psychological safety, can optimize the chances that real dangers will be recognized and addressed before it's too late. These conversations among individuals across all levels of the organization can empower companies to diligently institute novel approaches that enhance safety and profitability at the same time.

It's important to note, FedEx is not alone in this struggle. Employees for other major airfreight companies have died not only in frigid conditions but also in sweltering heat. Despite its longstanding approach to giving drivers full employment status, UPS has also encountered its own issues with how it treats employees. In 2016, a UPS driver nearly died as a result of a high-volume delivery day in the scorching summer heat in New Jersey. He had developed heatstroke, initially manifesting with nausea and vomiting. When the condition progressed, he ended up in the emergency room with dangerously low blood pressure and life-threatening kidney failure. Despite fifteen years of experience with how to deal with summer heat on the job (water, cool towels, rest periods), the driver had succumbed to the horrific work conditions.[24] UPS doesn't air-condition most of its loading docks and the cargo holds of its trucks, which reportedly can rise to above 140 degrees on the hottest days. This puts workers at undue risk, as rising temperatures lead to potentially deadly changes in vital signs and metabolic functions.

Whether the days are freezing cold or dangerously hot or anywhere in between, the major airfreight companies must continue to explore how to align their performance metrics with the health and safety of their workers. This endeavor, which requires equal focus on the corporate balance sheet and the wellness of workers, depends on a long-term commitment to active inquiry, psychologically safe conversations among key stakeholders, and innovations driven by the Think Talk Create process.

Social Capital

There are myriad examples of twenty-first-century companies that know they can do well by doing good—and they're not all manufacturers of herbal teas or yoga mats. Employing 117,000 people in its 340 grocery stores in Texas and northern Mexico, H-E-B is one of the most beloved and most successful companies in America, competing on price with Walmart and on quality with Whole Foods while growing by leaps and bounds. H-E-B's highly progressive policies—including extensive management training that helps employees advance their careers—create intense loyalty, and its community participation makes it a revered institution everywhere the company operates. H-E-B provides $30 million in product and transportation aid to support food banks each year, and it helps feed 250,000 people annually in a holiday Feast of Sharing.

Given that the company operates in a hurricane-prone region, it has a commitment to emergency management that we might say puts FEMA to shame. Running trucks out of an emergency management center, H-E-B delivered four million pounds of food and $1 million in financial aid to victims of Hurricanes Katrina and Rita. During Hurricane Harvey, employees served 50,000 meals out of the H-E-B mobile kitchen while delivering 150,000 cases of water, 75,000 bags of ice, and 4,000 bags of dog and cat food. In return, community members in many flooded areas pitched in to help protect their beloved H-E-B store with sandbags. That commitment is the kind of customer loyalty that any organization could envy.[25]

What's called the "Spirit of H-E-B" flows from CEO Charles Butt and dates back to the founding of the company by his grandmother more than a century ago. The spirit suffuses the entire corporate culture, down to the frontline workers who, like the greeters at Walmart, can make such a difference in people's lives. Even lower- and mid-level workers in major corporations can have a powerful influence on humanizing the workplace, the economy, and the orderly functioning of society. Social capital is harder to quantify than financial capital, but in the long run it may be even more important.

In the next chapter we'll explore, through a professional sports narrative, another example of how community engagement and attentiveness to all stakeholders builds positive feelings, loyalty, and the kind of business growth that the strict shareholder-value mindset overlooks entirely.

7

HOME ICE IS WHERE THE HEART IS

The Value of Playing in the Arena of Emotion

No business can get off the ground without customers who have a passion for the goods it serves up, often coupled with an emotional connection to the people who represent the brand. But as businesses mature into corporate entities, forming departmental structures and hiring people with specialized skills (but little care for what launched the business in the first place), customers can feel frozen out as the personal touch steadily disappears. It's a death by a thousand cuts. In the end, the long-standing customers, the ones who were most fired up and willing to spend, may be overlooked in favor of higher potential revenue from, well, somewhere—maybe in the big, bright city. The New York Islanders hockey franchise is a case in point, another example of an organization that was led astray by the numbers, when it needed to pay attention to the humans.

Professional hockey may seem an unlikely place to look for a lesson about active inquiry and Think Talk Create. Then again, who knows more about building brand loyalty and a rabid following than a pro sports team? What other product inspires thousands of people to paint their faces, wear crazy hats and vintage jerseys, and pay big money to crowd into an arena and scream themselves into exhaustion? The journey of the Islanders and their die-hard fans on Long Island over the last five decades speaks volumes about the emotional undercurrents that propel successful long-range business journeys.

After years of glory in the 1980s, the Islanders nearly went defunct under the weight of a corrupt owner in the 1990s (whose brief stint with the team led him to federal prison for bank and wire fraud). Under subsequent ownership, there was a failed attempt to construct a badly needed new arena. More recently, a Think Talk Create process between team ownership and members of the fan base, public officials, and other key stakeholders has, after years of struggle, ensured the team's ability to remain on Long Island and expand its cadre of fans. How did this narrative take such a positive turn? We can glimpse the renewed success and long-term hope for the Islanders through the lens of two of the team's youngest, most impassioned fans.

The Old Barn

"This is the rowdiest place I've ever seen!" Isaac shouted to his brother Elias, awestruck and heart pounding. "How could they even think about closing it down?"

The Islanders, bolstered by frenzied cheering, had just scored an amazing goal to win, by a score of three to two, the most remarkable game of the 2018–2019 National Hockey League season. It was the perfect fairy-tale homecoming. No one thought their beloved Islanders would ever be back in this building.

The Islanders' home ice was at Nassau Veterans Memorial Coliseum, which had opened in 1972. The location itself was on the grounds of Mitchel Field, an air base built in 1917 on wide open land on the Hempstead Plains of Long Island. It had been quietly operated by the US Air Force after the end of World War I, but in 1927 Charles Lindbergh entered Mitchel Field into the history books by taking off from there on his solo journey to Paris, the first ever transatlantic flight. By the 1940s, following the end of World War II, suburban communities were springing up all around the airfield, accommodating returning veterans and city dwellers seeking the American Dream out in the suburbs. In 1961, Mitchel Field closed after forty-three years of proud service. Eleven years later, the Nassau Coliseum opened. Then in 2015 it, too, closed after forty-three years.

The "Old Barn," as the locals called it, needed to be renovated or replaced. Instead, due to a complexity of financial and other factors, the team's owners decided to move their operations, and all of the team's home games, to a swanky new arena in downtown Brooklyn. Opened in 2012 as the home of the Brooklyn Nets of the NBA, and named after a powerful international bank, the Barclays Center had leather seats and corporate luxury suites. Nice for the expense-account crowd—Barclays lies just across the East River from Manhattan, a short subway ride away from the world's greatest media and financial hub. But luxurious amenities meant nothing to the Islanders' hard-core fans who, generally speaking, were on more of a hot-dog-and-beer budget.

Otherwise, the Barclays Center was a big hit. This was the first time since 1957, when the Dodgers baseball team ripped the heart out of Brooklyn by moving to Los Angeles, that a professional sports team would play in Brooklyn. Barclays also played host to major headline events, including wildly popular concerts by hip-hop artist and Brooklyn legend Jay-Z (who was a part owner of the Nets). For the Islanders, this seemed to be a step up to the big time, allowing them, after years as a "lunch box" team, to play their home games in a state-of-the-art facility.

This corporatization of sports—with naming rights, big TV contracts, and appeals to high rollers—began not long after the Nassau Coliseum was built. The arena sits right in the heart of modest, suburban Nassau County. It's only about thirty miles from Manhattan, but it exists in a different universe.

Fittingly, Manhattan has the world's most famous arena since ancient Rome: Madison Square Garden, home to the NHL's New York Rangers, one of the league's original six teams dating back to 1926. The Rangers, the Montreal Canadiens, the Boston Bruins, and the Chicago Blackhawks are the Goliaths of the NHL, and they play in the heart of the great North American financial centers. They have a long history of winning, and a long history of being highly profitable.

It's only natural that corporations would spend lots of money entertaining clients at sporting events; the downside is that the escalation in ticket prices has made these games unaffordable for most ordinary citizens. The middle-class experience of bringing the family out to the ballpark or the hockey rink has faded into a distant memory for many Americans. Slowly, over the last few decades, rowdy blue-collar fans have been replaced by far more reserved upper-middle-class professionals and business leaders. The cheering is not as loud or as colorful as it used to be. After all, when you're doing a deal in a sky box, who has time to actually watch the game?

The suburban Islanders, the David among the NHL's Goliaths, have been among the league's most under-resourced teams since their inception in 1972. They struggled mightily to develop a fan base in their first few years of play. In those early years, more Rangers fans than Islanders fans populated the Coliseum seats. People bought tickets to Islanders games not to see the Islanders, but to see visiting teams and hockey greats like Bobby Orr of the Bruins. These were big-time events in a small-time place, and usually there were plenty of empty seats on the arena's upper level. The hapless Islanders were the classic expansion team for the first couple of years, with a fan base that was pathetically small. This remained a discouraging fact until the team, under the steady and visionary direction of Bill Torrey ("the Architect," as he came to be known), soon began drafting and signing some of the most promising up-and-coming talent of the day, as well as one of the game's greatest coaches: Al Arbour.

Somehow, the Islanders racked up enough wins to make the playoffs in 1975. Hope and even passion for the team were in the air. That spring, the Islanders upset the powerful Rangers squad for their first playoff-series victory. Cars all over the Island suddenly sported bumper stickers reading "Lord Stanley Is Moving to Long Island," referring to the namesake of the NHL's Stanley Cup championship trophy. And the bumper-sticker premonition magically came true not too many years later. The Islanders stunned the sports world by winning the Stanley Cup championship in 1980 and then going on to win three more in '81, '82, and '83. Triumphant photos of the Islanders celebrating Cup victories appeared on the pages of *Sports Illustrated*. The team was now the pride of Long Island and its overlooked middle class and little-known towns. Many of the team's idolized players in those days now stand among the NHL's most admired Hall of Famers, including Denis Potvin, Bryan Trottier, and Mike Bossy.

People tend to think of Manhattan when they think of New York. But it's places like the Long Island suburbs, the backyard of the world's capital, where some of the last vestiges of American middle-class life survive. Blue-collar workers own houses. People still know their neighbors. They have block parties and take in each other's mail when someone goes away on vacation. The scores of towns and villages traversing Long Island lack the cosmopolitan feel and flair of contemporary Brooklyn and Manhattan, but they have many of the same problems that have migrated out into suburban and even rural areas in the twenty-first century: the opioid crisis, skyrocketing costs of living, and crumbling infrastructure. But for these folks just outside the glow of the big city's bright lights, at least they had their beloved Islanders.

All the more reason, then, that the Islanders' 2015 departure from the Coliseum to the faraway, impersonal, gentrifying center of Brooklyn was crushing. For many residents of the towns in easy driving distance of the old arena, it felt like a communal death blow that was stripping Long Island of its soul.

Even for Isaac and Elias, who were eleven and nine at the time, it was a moment of loss and sadness. Their love of scrappy hockey teams, and their bond with family, had initially sparked a remarkable interest in the Islanders—and they'd lived in Boston their entire lives! Their father had grown up in North Bellmore, a bike ride from the Coliseum and—unlike the nearby, more affluent towns of Roslyn and Great Neck—a place few people had ever heard of.

The boys' grandparents still lived in the house in North Bellmore that they had purchased in 1968, well before ground had even been broken on the Coliseum. The profound emotional bond to the team was entwined with family history, nostalgia, underdog status, and a host of other emotional driving forces.

When Isaac and Elias attended their first Islanders game in 2012, their grandparents' split-level house and the Nassau Coliseum looked essentially the same as they had back in the 1970s. For preadolescent boys intrigued by their family history, it was a source of fascination. On each visit, one by one, Isaac took his father's old Islanders shirts, banners, yearbooks, and memorabilia for his bedroom in Boston, which he was in the process of turning into an Islanders shrine. Isaac couldn't care less about corporate box sales at the Barclays Center, but he began to use his allowance to buy vintage Islanders collectibles on eBay. All he wanted for his birthday were Islanders tickets and memorabilia. He and his brother took road trips to see the team play in other cities, such as Columbus, Ohio, and Phoenix, Arizona. This is how undervalued teams like the Islanders can sell tickets and make ends meet. These are potent, emotion-driven business opportunities, rooted in people's love for family, nostalgia, and narrative.

Behavioral Economics

For sports teams like the Islanders, as for all businesses, awareness of the emotional dynamics of customers is a matter of life and death. Asking customers—in this case sports fans—what they care most about is essential. Isaac and Elias show that it's all about the emotions that well up and erupt to the surface, as was the case for the patient with abulia when he commented on Dr. Fisher's remarkable portrait at

Mass General. Ask these boys, and as many other die-hard Islanders fans as possible, where they think the team should play. Here is where active inquiry and behavioral economics are complementary and intertwined. Active inquiry serves a critical integrative function that marries raw emotion to rational financial decision-making. It builds upon, and moves beyond, behavioral economics by engaging customers in meaningful conversations about what they value. When people are asked open-ended questions about what's meaningful to them and what they really love, the floodgates open. If they feel heard and cared about, they buy.

Behavioral economics research has revealed that successful branding depends on forging an emotional bond with customers.[1] People make spending decisions based less on rational, numerical calculations than on intuitions, impressions, and feelings. The conventional microeconomics taught for many decades in university classrooms and applied in business settings has presumed the existence of rational humans whose decision-making and actions are grounded in analytical reasoning and logic. This predominant worldview has been upended in recent times. Richard Thaler, a professor at the University of Chicago's Booth School of Business, won a Nobel Prize in economics in 2017 for his groundbreaking research demonstrating the powerful role of emotion, even irrationality, when it comes to financial decision-making. Thaler's work is part of a wider intellectual movement originating with another Nobel Prize winner in economics, Daniel Kahneman. His book *Thinking,*

Fast and Slow exhaustively delineates much of the empirical research on the interplay of rationality and emotionality in economics.

Thaler and his colleagues, for example, had investigated whether the concept of fairness should play into the pricing decisions stores must make. In one of their studies, they looked into optimal pricing of snow shovels during major storms.[2] Traditional microeconomics, rooted in a quantitative analysis of supply and demand, would suggest that stores increase earnings by raising prices on shovels when there is heavy snow. But breeding long-term trust and emotional connection with customers should, and often does, dictate against this. Many small stores and even big-box stores like Walmart and Home Depot have learned that they should provide supplies like this at discounted prices (or even for free) during major storms. Besides being kind and community-oriented, this gesture creates goodwill that is likely to result in increased sales at a later date, as people associate the brand with desirable feelings of warmth and generosity.

In a 2018 article in the *American Economic Review*, Thaler describes how pure quantitative analysis reveals little about people's financial choices.[3] He recounts how a friend of his decades earlier had purchased many bottles of fine wine for around $5 apiece. The bottles subsequently increased in value by about twentyfold, outstripping the pace of inflation during those years. But instead of selling the bottles, his friend held on to them as collector's items and savored imbibing them on special occasions. Thaler observes that his friend would neither sell nor buy the bottles for $100 at that point in time. Buying them at $100 would feel like a bad deal on meaningless items disconnected from any personal history, while selling them at that price point would induce a profound sense of loss and regret about giving up prized trophies. Traditional numbers-based microeconomic theory could not explain this common phenomenon; it took a radical, new emotion-driven behavioral economics to capture it adequately.

A forceful wave of economic science continues to show that rational self-interest, a term widely used by mid-twentieth-century economists, usually does not explain human decision-making. We are remarkably social creatures whose choices are more likely to be driven by interpersonal needs and subconscious, often irrational, dynamics. Purely logic-based, quantitative reasoning can be limiting, even destructive, in organizations and relationships more generally. The groundbreaking neuroeconomics research of Paul Zak, as we have seen, reveals that collaboration and trust among stakeholders are key. Relational connectedness is the primary predictor of success among colleagues. It is also essential in fostering positive, loyal, and lucrative relationships with customers—such as those impassioned New York Islanders fans.

Long Island Iced Glee

Islanders management clearly hadn't been able to act on the powerful findings of behavioral economists. When in 2015 they moved the team to a geographically and emotionally distant region far from the fan base, everything declined. Average attendance at Barclays Center games sagged to the lowest in the NHL.[4] The fan experience in Brooklyn was dismal. Getting there and back required a long and harrowing ride on the cattle cars of the Long Island Rail Road or a frustrating, traffic-heavy drive and prohibitively expensive parking. Built for basketball, Barclays had many obstructed-view seats for hockey games, from which fans, who had paid astronomical ticket prices, couldn't see all the ice. The scoreboard hung nicely at the center of the basketball parquet floor, but it was off-center when the arena was turned into an ice rink—which, because of the arena's orientation and seating structure, needed to be placed awkwardly off to one side. Ice quality was poor and a source of constant complaint from players.

Die-hard fans like Isaac and Elias still adored the team, but they felt differently toward Islanders management. Billboards along the suburban highways of Long Island called for the removal of the team's general manager. Locals clamored for the Islanders' return to the Coliseum, but the NHL still saw the prospect of greater financial returns in Brooklyn. NHL leadership, particularly its commissioner, Gary Bettman, stated repeatedly and unequivocally that the Coliseum did not meet modern-day NHL arena standards.[5] It only had one concourse and far too few bathrooms to accommodate a capacity crowd. The 2015 renovation had made the place feel somewhat more comfortable and spread out, but it

reduced the seating to a subpar 13,900. Its architecture pre-
cluded construction of a sufficient number of luxury boxes
to drive profit for the team and the NHL. Bettman crushed
the Long Island fan base with his announcement that the
Islanders would never again play a game in the Old Barn.

When in mid-2018 the Islanders failed to renew the
contract of megastar John Tavares, things appeared to have
sunk to the lowest possible point for the franchise. Tavares, perhaps the league's best center, had made a staggering, emotion-based decision. Even though the Islanders
had offered him a contract worth over $88 million to stay
for the next eight years, he decided to accept a less financially favorable offer of $77 million from the Toronto Ma-
ple Leafs.[6] Logical calculations based on the numbers didn't
predict the outcome here, but once again the principles of
behavioral economics appeared to be on point. On the day
he announced his departure from New York and a return to
his boyhood home across the northern border in Ontario,
Tavares tweeted a childhood photo of himself asleep in his
bed, cozily wrapped in a Maple Leafs comforter. Feelings
and nostalgia, not financials, had driven one of the most
transformative decisions the twenty-nine-year-old all-star
had ever made. He was going home.

With the ongoing decline of the Islanders franchise and
vociferous protests from fans, the team owners and NHL
executives finally began to take serious note of the problems.
Economic calculations about luxury boxes and corporate engagement with the team had led nowhere, and neglect of

the core fan base out in the suburbs had taken its toll. The strategic plan for the urbanization of the Islanders had been a resounding failure. The owners had to take note of the behavioral economics at play, as the sad numbers were undeniable. Key performance indicators of financial success were awful. Signs of a shift back to Long Island began to appear in articles in *Newsday*, the Long Island newspaper that on May 25, 1980, had proudly featured the Islanders' first Stanley Cup win on its cover. The Sunday paper had cost 65 cents back then. A framed copy of that front page, with a beaming Potvin holding the Cup high, hung prominently in Isaac's bedroom in Boston.

With some degree of foresight, the Islanders in 2016 had purchased a training facility, the Northwell Health Ice Center, for the team in Eisenhower Park, about a half mile from the Coliseum. Plaques and banners from the good old days of the early 1980s adorned the building. It was open daily for community skating, and it hosted youth hockey tournaments. It had become one of Isaac and Elias's favorite destinations when visiting New York. You could get close to players here in a way that was common in the old days of professional sports but rare in the twenty-first century. Fans could see the team going in and out for practices and get autographs.

The boys succeeded in getting their grandmother to spend an inordinate fraction of her Social Security check on Islanders jerseys and other swag from the team shop— spending choices guided more by feelings than by numerical calculations and rational self-interest. She spent this money enthusiastically, relishing both her grandsons' delight and her memories of their father's boyhood Islanders obsession back in the '70s and '80s.

The quiet success of the Northwell facility was a forerunner of the team's return to its roots. Frustrated by the debacle in Brooklyn, team owners sought an alternative venue for the Islanders that would bring them back to their hungry fan base and also be economically viable for both the team and the NHL. The NHL had stated clearly that the Coliseum was no longer an option. The team would need a new home, and it wasn't immediately clear where that would be. Where else in the overdeveloped region would there be enough open land for suburbanites to drive, park easily, and tailgate before Islanders games? Raucous pregame tailgate barbecues and beer fests in the Coliseum parking lot had been a joyous staple of the Islanders experience for decades. It harkened back to the days before the NHL, like so many other professional sports leagues, had been scrubbed clean and turned into a sterile experience for the rich.

Islanders ownership wisely began tuning in to the human dimension, listening closely to fans. Islanders co-owner Jon Ledecky, with his naturally warm and boyish smile, began an active inquiry process with the team's fans. Wearing his expensive suits while fans sported team jerseys, Ledecky boarded Long Island Rail Road trains to talk intimately with the real people riding into and out of Brooklyn for games at

Barclays. Video clips of Ledecky's friendly and engaging interactions started to appear on YouTube and Twitter.

When Ledecky openly asked them about their experience attending games in Brooklyn versus on the Island, the fans gave him an earful, and he took it all in with a kind and earnest demeanor. This was active inquiry at its best. When fans told him how they admired the Islanders greats of yesteryear, he would offer to call the players and turn the phone over to fans to have a conversation with these heroes from the '70s and '80s. In one clip on Twitter, a middle-aged woman is seen chatting exuberantly on Ledecky's phone with Ed Westfall, the team's first captain. Ledecky was brilliantly engaging in the Think Talk Create process on the LIRR. With great care and thoughtfulness, he was laying the foundation for a renewal of the team's relationship with the fans who would guarantee its financial viability and community bonds for years to come.

Then, in 2018, like a deus ex machina dropping onto the stage, the governor of New York made an appearance in the unfolding drama. Andrew Cuomo publicly recalled warm personal memories of the Islanders dynasty in the early 1980s. A son of a former New York governor (Mario Cuomo) and brother of a well-known CNN news anchor (Chris Cuomo), Andrew Cuomo had grown up in Queens, the sole borough of New York City that borders Nassau County.

Governor Cuomo realized that, unlike the heavily liberal city, Long Island does not reliably elect Democrats. Its voting patterns are more like those of the middle-American Rust Belt. So, beyond his nostalgic bond to the team, Cuomo may have seen the opportunity here to connect with swing voters out on the Island. Then, like Ledecky, he engaged in an active inquiry process, talking tirelessly to stakeholders and inquiring into how team owners, investors, civic leaders, local politicians, and the NHL could bring the Islanders home to Long Island. Most important, perhaps, was the fact that Cuomo simply showed up. He attended meetings and gave speeches where his emotional connectedness was apparent. His eyes lit up when talking about the prospect of bringing the Islanders home. It was clear that it felt personal for him, that he could feel it in his heart. The governor wasn't only trying to complete a task, or garner votes for his reelection, or get something off his plate. His enthusiastic leadership presence was the main driving force.

Cuomo helped to broker a deal in which the NHL would allow the Islanders to play half of their home games in the Old Barn, starting the following season and continuing for at least a couple of years beyond that. This was cause for celebration in Nassau and Suffolk. But Cuomo also announced that the Islanders were the winners of a competitive bid (against New York's professional soccer team) to build their own brand-new facility in Elmont, a Nassau County town immediately abutting his home borough of Queens.[7] Revealing the power of behavioral economics—and showcasing how Think Talk Create can work—this elegant decision wove together emotions and numerical calculations.

Islanders fans could experience a glorious return of the team to Nassau County. They would see local Nassau County police, not the NYPD, patrolling the parking lots and concourses. They could tailgate once again before games. The menacing yet endearing singing of their made-up trope—"Don't mess with Long Island"—would once again boom through the arena and be geographically honest. At the same time, the Islanders would get the financial boost that was likely to result from a modern arena, adhering to contemporary NHL standards and constructed exclusively for the team. The ice quality would be prime, and the scoreboard would definitely hang at center ice. The sight lines from the seats to the rink would be perfect.

The new arena would have to go through major environmental impact studies before receiving final approval, and it would take at least three years to build. The residents of the quiet village of Elmont would need to be persuaded and reassured that the inevitable traffic jams for forty-one home games (and maybe additional playoff games) would be worth it. This was no longer the world of Robert Moses, the twentieth-century power broker who strong-armed politicians and ignored public opposition to build the great public works (like parkways and bridges) that have shaped the landscape of the New York metropolitan area. It would not be easy to make the new arena a reality. Since 1905, Elmont has been home to the famed Belmont racetrack, the site of the third and final leg of thoroughbred horse racing's most prized competition. Elmont residents were used to dealing with large crowds only once a year, in June, when the Belmont Stakes follows the Kentucky Derby and the Preakness.

The new Islanders arena was to be built on state-owned land immediately adjacent to the racetrack. It would tie the Islanders to the international greatness of the Belmont Stakes, while maintaining their roots in the modest Long Island suburbs. But between 2018 and 2021, the target date for the ribbon cutting at their future home, the Islanders were to play approximately half their games back at the Old Barn. Cuomo's influence over the NHL was widely lauded across Long Island.

Since 2015, the team had only played one preseason game at the Coliseum, against the Philadelphia Flyers in September 2017. In most cases, preseason games get little to no attention, and most seats remain empty. But that one seemingly meaningless game was a sellout. The *Newsday* headline on the following day was "Islanders' Return to Nassau Coliseum Creates Playoff Atmosphere."[8] Isaac and Elias were there with their eighty-three-year-old grandfather; it would be his last time attending a live sporting event before congestive heart failure landed him in assisted living (and then ended his life in 2019). The boys would later recall how he walked into the Coliseum that day with more energy and delight than they had seen in him for years.

In early December 2018, the Islanders played their much-anticipated first regular season game back at the Coliseum. A *New York Times* sports-page headline read, "Islanders Return to Nassau Coliseum, Thrilling Fans and Players

Alike," with the article noting that "fans celebrated in the most appropriate way possible: with a tailgate and a raucous comeback victory."[9] The enthusiasm surrounding the Islanders began to skyrocket. The return to the Coliseum had an uncanny, even alchemical, feel. "Going to Barclays Center, you feel like a stranger in someone's house," a fan told the *Times*, speaking for so many others. "Here, even before you walk in that building, you're home."

The team responded to the infusion of Coliseum energy by going on one of their greatest winning sprees since the 1980s. Their coach, Barry Trotz, commented that the deafening noise in the Coliseum, starting with warm-ups and continuing uninterrupted through all three periods of play, was so startling and intimidating to visiting players that it probably in itself was worth six additional wins for the season. The Coliseum magic now even seemed to carry over to the team's play at Barclays, where attendance was improving and the atmosphere intensifying, despite all the shortcomings of the Brooklyn venue as a hockey arena.

The team was on a tear, and fans now wanted more. As it became clear that the Islanders were going to make the playoffs for the first time in three years, the burning question became whether home playoff games would be held at Barclays or at the Coliseum. The NHL consistently hits pay dirt each spring with universally sold-out, nationally televised matches. Islanders ownership and NHL leadership understandably wanted to capitalize financially on a playoff series. Barclays had more seats and revenue-generating luxury boxes. From a microeconomics perspective, Barclays seemed the obvious choice. But everyone knew that one of the main reasons the Islanders were surging was their return to the Coliseum and reconnection with their fan base. How incredible would it be for fans to watch the Islanders hoist a Stanley Cup trophy above their heads in 2019 in the same building where Potvin had first done so in 1980?

Once again, Islanders leadership and NHL corporate faced a dilemma and needed to make a complex business decision quickly. Would the emotionality of the Coliseum win out over the potential, but still uncertain, financial upside at Barclays? In mid-February 2019, the league made a much-awaited announcement. The Islanders would play the first playoff round at the Coliseum and, if they were to advance, the remainder of their playoff home games in Brooklyn. A compromise had been struck. Fans would experience the unforeseen return of playoff games to the Coliseum. They celebrated this aspect of the decision as a victory. But in 2019 they would not have any chance of seeing a final Cup game in the Old Barn. The moneymakers would probably make more money at Barclays, so local fans would have to hope and pray that the force field around the Coliseum would carry thirty miles into downtown Brooklyn, powering the team to progress deep into the playoffs.

Throughout the 2018–2019 season, the remarkable socioeconomic dynamics of hockey in the New York area remained just as visible as they had always been. Despite the fact that the Rangers were having a miserable season and weren't in contention for a playoff spot, they remained the primary target of taunts and chants at the two Islanders home arenas. Fans were thrilled to watch the Rangers falter and not even come close to making it into the playoffs.

The Islanders, on the other hand, ended the regular season in rousing fashion. Although they fell just one point short of winning their division title, the Islanders' second-place finish was enough to ensure them home-ice advantage for the first round of the playoffs. That meant the first two games of their best-of-seven playoff series, against the formidable Pittsburgh Penguins, would take place at the Coliseum. Game five, if no team had swept the first four, would be there as well. And if the series progressed to three wins apiece, the decisive game seven would also be at the Old Barn. Not since 1988 had the Islanders secured home-ice advantage for a playoff series. It was a fitting end to an inspiring 2018–2019 regular season.

What happened next seemed so predictable and scripted that it rose to the level of a cliché sports movie. The Islanders defeated the Penguins in the first two games at the Coliseum and the next two games in Pittsburgh for a decisive four-game sweep. The energy of the Old Barn was continuing to work its way into the postseason. Now came the Eastern Conference semifinals against the Carolina Hurricanes, a wild-card team that had nearly missed a playoff berth. The Islanders had home ice in name only, as games one and two were to be held in Brooklyn. They lost both of those games and dropped the next two in Raleigh. It was hardly debatable that the move to Barclays, a quantitative decision imposed by the NHL, had sent the momentum in the wrong direction for the team. A Hurricanes player confirmed the point in no uncertain terms. As the series was coming to a close, a *Newsday* headline read: "Ex-Islander Calvin de Haan Says Hurricanes Benefited from Avoiding Nassau Coliseum."[10] The playoff departure from the Old Barn was as remarkable as the return to it had been in the middle of the regular season.

History and Heart

Aside from the Islanders' journey, the Coliseum story continued to evolve during these years, reflecting the tension between corporate interests and local traditions. The 2015 renovation had resulted in the Coliseum being renamed NYCB Live: Home of the Nassau Veterans Memorial Coliseum. NYCB is short for New York Community Bank, the spiffed-up arena's primary corporate sponsor. This awkward step toward mainstream branding smacked of old-school microeconomics: advertise and you'll bring in more business. But no one on Long Island was about to refer to the arena that way, except in jest. It remained "the Coliseum" or "the Old Barn" both in ordinary conversations and on TV broadcasts. When the free T-shirts tossed to fans during breaks in play turned out to have the NYCB Live logo on them, rather than the team logo, Isaac and Elias simply rolled their eyes. It was apparent that no one in NYCB's marketing department was doing active inquiry with the Islanders' fan base. The misguided naming decision for the arena, combined with event cancellations during the pandemic, led to the termination of the NYCB naming agreement in 2020.

The Nassau Veterans Memorial Coliseum commemorates the honor and sacrifices of the twentieth-century US military, from World War I through Vietnam. It was named in honor of the nation's veterans, even at a time when the country was in strife and downtrodden by the Vietnam experience—and generally not treating its returning veterans with the dignity they deserved. County officials had the good judgment and foresight to require that the building maintain its name to honor veterans. When NYCB became the corporate sponsor in 2015, the company followed this rule but subordinated the long-standing name to a mere subheading in small print. It appeared to be just a matter of compliance, not a matter of respect. Other parts of the Mitchel Field site—including the old airplane hangars that have been converted into the Cradle of Aviation Museum—continue to recognize and celebrate the history of the place, even as NYCB went in a different direction. But young people in the twenty-first century have become highly sensitized to corporate values and responsibility. "I'd never give my money to NYCB. They don't get it about the Islanders," Isaac said. "It's all about history and heart."

For many years before the 2015 renovation made way for NYCB Live, large signs had ringed the outside of the Coliseum, reading "We Are All Islanders." The double meaning evoked the sense of connectedness that the team inspired, the glue that held Long Island together in an increasingly fragmented world. Corporate and financial interests drove the team from what we might think of as its preindustrial old barn into a twenty-first-century cathedral of capitalism and return on investment. But a myriad of examples demonstrate that such changes can come at a high cost. A team owner and a governor who engaged in active inquiry with fans and other stakeholders appear to have saved the day.

The Islanders are moving back to Long Island and their gritty fan base, now with a modern arena right on the geographic and spiritual edge of New York City. UBS, the multinational Swiss bank, has purchased the naming rights for the arena—and hopefully will learn from and avoid the missteps of NYCB. UBS would do well to send its leaders and representatives into the villages of Long Island to talk with fans about how the bank can serve and inspire the community in the years to come. Perhaps the marriage of Old Barn and Big Bank values will help to bring the team, and the wider world of sports and work, toward a more rewarding and sustainable equilibrium.

8

THE NEW MBA: MASTER OF BUSINESS AMELIORATION

Adopting a New Philosophy of Business

H-E-B and the New York Islanders are prime examples of the truth that exclusive attention to shareholder value isn't the only way for businesses to succeed. If the ideas of Friedman and Jensen can infiltrate our professional psyche, so, too, can active inquiry and Think Talk Create. It's a win-win scenario for businesses looking to grow and for the people who work in those businesses. That's because it's their collaborative ideas, their strategies, their efforts, and their motivations that will determine whether the business will flourish, or if it will temporarily extract value like a social and fiscal parasite.

If quantitative, bottom-line thinking can be taught and implemented to the benefit of the few, so can active inquiry to the benefit of us all. There are already changes afoot in business schools that may help to move us into a post-shareholder-value-only world. New graduates are making pivotal choices about how to conduct themselves in the business and professional worlds of the twenty-first century.

Commencement

When people graduate from colleges and universities, full of new and up-to-date knowledge, they step into the outside world hoping to make a difference. This is, in part, why convocations can be so inspiring. Gowns, robes, and pomp and circumstance combine on a weekend afternoon in the spring or early summer to recognize another year of wide-eyed future lawyers, doctors, businesspeople, politicians, accountants, and academics. Graduation signals to the world the release of a new pool of (hopefully) well-prepared individuals ready, willing, and able to tackle society's greatest challenges.

Graduation ceremonies symbolically mark the moment of transition between pre-enlightened and enlightened. That transition, of course, is meant to have taken place over the period of time each student was enrolled at the university. But the precise instant when the degrees are conferred is a bar or bat mitzvah of sorts; supposedly, from this point on, you're a grown-up. Like the flick of a switch, you have instantly transformed from childhood to adulthood or, in the case of graduation, from one who is unknowing to one who is knowing.

Convocation ceremonies at our alma mater, the University of Chicago, are orchestrated in the center of the main quad. Surrounded by neo-Gothic architecture, candidates for graduation sit in folding chairs, facing an improvised stage on which professors, honorary degree recipients, and university administrators draped in flowing robes are arrayed like a massive choir about to perform a concert of secular hymns. The symbolism inspires hope that hard work and learning are still respected and valued. We have both had the experience of graduating from the University of Chicago and participating in the convocation ceremonies there. Now, living in New England, we get the same hopeful feeling each time we walk past the stately Boston Public Library and read the inscription engraved in large lettering beneath the cornice on one side of the building: "The Commonwealth requires the education of the people as the safeguard of order and liberty."

At a recent University of Chicago graduation, department chairs and academic deans stood before the microphone and asked all candidates under their supervision to please stand and be recognized by the university president. Once the degrees were conferred, each of these divisions then received a special message from the president about how he and the broader university hope their degrees will be put to use. It's one of the few times that academic leadership these days guides people toward a shared sense of value and purpose.

For graduates in the social and physical sciences, the president always says something to the effect of "May you enrich the knowledge and practice of your chosen field." For students graduating with a degree in fine arts, the president warmly states, "May your work enhance our artistic and cultural landscape." This goes on and on throughout the proceedings with little fanfare, as his hopeful messages seldom receive much audible response from the crowd. That is until the dean from the school of business takes the podium and presents candidates for the degree of master of business administration. The president extends a wish, with no apparent sense of irony, that these newly anointed MBA degrees be put to the purpose of "responsible development of international business for the benefit of all people." The remark prompts a few eye rolls and quiet chuckles from the audience.

It was right around the height of the commencement season in 2019 that the United Nations released the study saying that the "relentless global pursuit of economic growth is driving the collapse of life on earth."[1] Perhaps it is because of this evidence, coupled with the anxiously vague well-wishes of a university president, that the mood in some management programs has begun to shift away from the ideas of Friedman and Jensen. Nitin Nohria, dean of Harvard Business School, noted in a recent *Economist* interview that more and more incoming students want their future employers to reflect "purpose and values" in their organizational behavior and mission.[2] They are looking to work for companies that are as serious about developing social capital as they are about financial capital.

Many business school students have turned their focus back to the humanistic considerations behind the numbers that loom so large in their training. If they were medical students, they would have been the ones to lean down and empathetically ask the open-ended question—"How was that for you?"—that Dr. Fisher left out of his conversation with the man suffering from abulia. They may have done much more than apply a depression rating scale to Ramon. They may have cut Marc a break and let him attend his daughter's wedding without undue stress. As MBAs, they now may ask open-ended questions of each other and themselves about how to put quantitative data, coupled with the core principles of capitalism, to use for the greater good.

Adjusting to this palpable social current of the early twenty-first century, other leading institutions have taken similar steps. William Boulding, dean of Duke's Fuqua School of Business, encourages his students "to be thoughtful about the role of business in society." This has given rise to a new task for MBA programs around the globe. Not only must they educate students in the language of business and in the technical skills of accounting and financial modeling, but they also must educate them to recognize the myriad potential outcomes and consequences of corporate actions for the staff, customers, and other stakeholders—including dire consequences like a growing number of employee deaths (some by suicide and even more by stress-induced illnesses) and the potential mass extinction of a million species. A new generation has entered the business world and observed the areas in the brick wall of business-as-usual that are in dire need of reshaping.

These MBA students are certainly going to make up future management tiers, but even in the early stages of their career they are far from alone in their expectations. More and more employees seek purpose and values from their workplace, regardless of age and seniority within the company. In short, it's not just those pesky millennials. Nearly half of the workforce—around 42 percent—reports that it's a priority to work for an organization that has a positive impact on the world.[3] Whether they are young and entering business school, or more established, or even nearing retirement, a significant percentage of people want to work for an organization whose values match their own.

You Have a Choice

According to the *Harvard Business Review*, some companies understand that employees are as important as the paying customers who consume the products and services they sell.[4] A handful of prominent organizations have taken note. Unilever, for example, has promised to reduce its environmental footprint and increase its positive impact on society. As a result of its humanistic shift, the company reported that half of its new applicants "cite the company's ethical approach and sustainability work as the primary reason they want to work for the company."[5]

Yet in spite of this positive trend, other companies are reluctant to make that kind of commitment, so much so that, according to a recent Gallup poll, only 27 percent of employees say they believe in their company's values.[6] That's a sobering statistic. Think if you were to conduct a quick survey over lunch one day by asking colleagues whether they believe in the lofty values cited in your mission statement. Chances are that a considerable number—perhaps three out of four—will say they do not. That means, in the eyes of employees, even companies that profess some socially oriented purpose and values are seen as just mouthing platitudes.

This all stands in telling contrast to findings made by the National Bureau of Economic Research. A team there interviewed 1,348 companies across North America and found that 92 percent of CEOs said improving their company's culture would increase the company's overall value. Plus, only 16 percent of those CEOs believed their company's culture was where it needed to be.[7] Yet, in spite of this admission, employees aren't seeing a change. Other reports have shown that nearly 45 percent of team members believe senior leadership is minimally if at all committed to improving their respective organization's culture.[8]

Stepping outside of the C-suite in this way, a number of firms have proactively tried to conduct these official yet anonymous watercooler surveys. For example, nationally representative studies have shown that those pesky millennials, who are thought to be so different from everybody else, aren't so different after all. Per research, "Millennials, Baby Boomers, and Gen Xers have the same core work values— and tend to rank them in the same order of importance."[9] The young MBA students seeking purpose and value from their employers really just want the same thing as everyone else: to leave the world a little better off than when they got here. They are very adept with new technology, but they almost never mention it as the main reason they get out of bed and go to work each day.

This emerging workforce not only wants to join an organization with purpose and values, but, according to *The 2017 Deloitte Millennial Survey*, they also feel they can exert more influence on the world's biggest problems via the workplace.[10] In other words, for those surveyed, their job and the organization they work for is the vehicle through which they hope to enact positive change. These emerging recruits will be able to do so only if they can work with flexibility in psychologically safe environments, where they can engage in active inquiry and address the big picture, looking at how empirical evidence and data might drive not only shareholder value but, more importantly, shared values.

Open discussions around this topic—what's the highest good for the human community and the world we must inhabit together—are good for business and may well be the salvation of the capitalist system. As businesses take note of the empirically proven positive impact of a trusting and psychologically safe work environment, they will want to hire and promote individuals who are masters of the age-old process of active inquiry. Ancient Greek philosophy isn't dead. In fact, we can make excellent use of it to enliven the modern-day workplace. And that's why Socrates should get a raise instead of a bowl of hemlock.

Business schools can lead the way forward. In a conversation with us, William Boulding of the Fuqua School of Business—which is at the forefront of developing leaders uniquely capable of tackling twenty-first-century challenges—acknowledged the remarkable shift away from the Friedman and Jensen mindset. "The reality of capitalism is that it has been one of the most powerfully positive forces in history," he told us. "We want to be sure our students think deeply and are motivated with good intentions about the positive impact of business in society. But," he added, "they need to understand how they want to operate." Consequently, he said it is a new responsibility of business schools to "help students understand meaning, purpose, and both the qualitative and quantitative impact of their decision-making." As dean, he considers it his responsibility to help students by providing them with "frameworks for making choices."[11]

Marianne Bertrand, a professor of economics at the University of Chicago's Booth School of Business, considers the subject of economics to be the study of how people, and the companies they work for, make choices within a set of limitations. Sometimes these choices have to do with buying an apple instead of an orange, and other times they carry greater personal significance, as when a graduate chooses which first job to take or when an executive chooses whether to provide employees with a reasonable benefit package and a flexible work schedule. We're inundated with choice daily, from granular, low-stakes decisions to much larger, more substantive choices.

Behavioral economics, as we've seen, teaches us that our choices aren't driven by rational self-interest nearly as much as we once presumed; they aren't determined or dictated by pure quantitative analysis. It's our human emotions and social networks that carry the day. So we had better develop enough self-reflective capacity to understand those emotions and how to employ them for both the highest good and the bottom line. For this, we depend on the integrative functions of our frontal lobes, the biological seat of executive functioning and sound decision-making.

During a rainy June afternoon on Chicago's South Side, Bertrand joined the university president onstage along with her fellow educators for the 2018 convocation ceremony in Hyde Park. But before the university president could extend his specific departmental wishes for all degree recipients, and before the audience could subtly chuckle at his perhaps not-so-Pollyannaish hopes for the MBA students to pursue the "responsible development of international business," Bertrand stepped up to the podium.

She was asked to deliver that year's convocation address—a prestigious invitation from the university to a distinguished member of its faculty that replaces the celebrity guest-speaker portion of many graduation ceremonies at other institutions. As we all know, graduation speeches are, almost invariably, warm and optimistic. They are adorned with platitudes and Winston Churchill quotes and important lessons about the places this graduating class will go. Some are memorable, but many lack impact for the simple reason that they are all just so overwhelmingly similar in their content and message. This one was distinctive. Bertrand offered a novel message to the audience that day, especially to her students graduating from the business school:

> If you are graduating with an economics degree or business degree—or really any degree—I sure hope that you understand that misleading and cheating should never be part of your job description. Nothing good happens, either to our economy or our society, when businesses flourish because they cheat, while other businesses struggle because they remain honest. And yes, you have a choice. You can exert voice—be an active agent for cultural change when you see this culture lacking at your place of employment. You can also vote with your feet and exit if the culture is not right and not fixable.[12]

Her address is important for a number of reasons, not the least of which is her matter-of-fact remark: "You have a choice." There is often a sense of hopelessness, of inadequacy, of powerlessness when looking at your broader organization as a harshly quantitative, bottom-line-oriented entity. It can feel a bit like being in a canoe beside a massive cruise ship. There is nothing you can do, from your tiny wooden toy, to alter the course of this behemoth. It might turn just a few degrees, upending your canoe and putting you at risk of drowning. But what we lose sight of is the reality that organizations are not entities unto themselves. They are not cruise ships, and they don't have to be the *Titanic* on its ill-fated course. We all can play a role in steering them.

You Are the Company

Business is not an inherent force in the universe; business is what we make it. How many times must we hear the adage "It's not personal; it's just business" before we are forced to grab the shoulders of the person before us and gently shake them until they understand that business is only personal, and it should be anything but inhumane? An insurance company firing a veteran employee like Marc one day before he is able to collect retirement benefits or pensions being wiped out for thousands of loyal team members has a profound personal impact. They are decisions made by one person that affect others in significant ways. Robbing employees of their financial security is business according to whom? It is only business according to that person who either has not yet realized their agency and choice in the matter or, more terrifyingly, has realized their agency but is reluctant to change the inhumanity of their ways.

Think back to how Jay, a mid-level employee sitting in a cubicle of the impersonal offices of a major insurance company, did the right thing morally and financially by ensuring that a maimed boy would receive the funds he deserved—all while maintaining the health and credibility of his company. Or how the custodians at the property-management firm defined a different kind of C-suite—the caring suite—by including their humanistic perspective on the residents at the assisted-living facility. The momentous choices of the little guy can have an outsize impact on the integrity and profitability of companies and organizations of every stripe and size. A company without its component parts—its employees—is not out there bouncing aimlessly in the ocean, its navigators only looking for a horizon representing the bottom line. A company is simply a group of people working toward common ends that inevitably weave together into one broad human objective.

In the language of seventeenth-century philosopher Thomas Hobbes, we might think of a company as the Leviathan: a gargantuan entity composed entirely of individuals who enter into a social contract with one another for their mutual support and care. In the Hobbesian state of nature, unchecked aggression creates a dangerous free-for-all, with each individual looking out for his or her own self-interest. It's a world where amygdala hijack predominates. To survive and succeed, we need to talk to each other more, collaborate, and find safety in a shared world. As long as one person is deprived of the opportunity to enter into that social contract, we are all at risk and we cannot thrive. We all must reach toward joining the Leviathan as productive members of the human community, even when it seems difficult or impossible. Without a mindset that it really is possible, we are doomed to dehumanization and loss.

Without people, a company doesn't exist, because a company is its people. We once had a conversation with a friend, a public-facing executive, who was disappointed with her organization's stuffy culture. She kept saying things like, "I don't know what the company would think" and "How would the company react?" After a short while we stopped and reminded her: "You are the company!" Then we did some casual, but we hope meaningful, active inquiry with her. In what way, even a small one, can you influence the corporate culture? When you make that presentation next week, what can you include on a PowerPoint slide that reflects your sense of what's right? What can you say and do that will empower you to shape the company's approach to better serving its customers? What aspirational thoughts would help you feel like you're not a cog in a motor running out of your control?

When preparing for his high-wire walk between the World Trade Center towers in 1974, Philippe Petit was told by one of his team members, "You can't do this. It's impossible." To which Petit responded, "Yes, of course it's impossible. So how do we do it?"[13] His feat was chronicled in the 2008 film *Man on Wire*, which won the Academy Award the following year for Best Documentary Feature. Walking across the World Trade Center towers on a high wire—illegally, and without safety gear—was seemingly impossible, but in fact Petit did it. It's just an inspiring reminder of what we're all capable of in some way.

It is our underlying cognitions about who we are that largely determine how we act in that world. This was an idea presented, in large part, by William James, who wrote in an

1870 diary entry: "My first act of free will shall be to believe in free will."[14] Urban legend tells of a story in which James was asked to deliver a lengthy speech in front of a crowd of academics and researchers eager to hear his thoughts on the history of psychology. Settled in for an extensive report, the crowd was shocked by James's choice to speak for just a few seconds. "They've asked me to talk about the last hundred years of psychological research," he is said to have told them. "It can be summed up in this statement: people by and large become what they think of themselves. Thank you and good night."

James expanded further upon this idea of belief in oneself during another lecture entitled "The Will to Believe," which was published as a book in 1896. According to James, the belief "I am capable of changing the world" can only be true—or become true—if you first adopt the belief without prior evidence.[15] In other words, assuming you haven't changed the world yet, the first step in doing so is believing strongly that you can.

No matter how large or small, or how famous or infamous, companies, organizations, nonprofits, universities, and even governments are, they are nothing more than a collective of individuals acting on behalf of—or in the name of—a branded entity. When we feel most daunted by the mere notion of having an influence in these scenarios, we may reflect on William James's "will to believe," which can be understood as a volitional open-mindedness to possibilities. It requires a self-disciplined decision to make hypotheses about a desired, and not implausible, truth. In interpersonal scenarios, James notes, there are many "cases where a fact cannot come at all unless preliminary faith exists in its coming."

A simple example is Congress. If your morning newspaper or favorite news site mentions a decision (or lack thereof) made by "Congress," remember that Congress didn't make a decision. Congress is incapable of making a decision precisely because it's not a person. Individuals make up Congress, and it is the individuals who collectively make decisions in its name. The American government is a version of the Leviathan. If and when it ever functions properly, its representatives will put aside their rational self-interest and poll numbers in order to reach toward a broader vision of what America can and should be. They will think, talk, and create a better union. In the midst of the COVID-19 crisis and an ongoing struggle toward achieving a more just society, we have never needed the Think Talk Create model more.

In the late eighteenth century, as the Founding Fathers were piecing together a government, they conceived of a central Treasury Department and a financial system that assumed the debts that the states had accrued during the Revolutionary War. However, it wasn't "the government" that created this system; it was Alexander Hamilton acting on behalf of, and in the name of, the government. He, as an individual person, made the choices necessary to ensure the new country's economic security. The perspective that an organization is an entity unto itself, capable of making its own choices, is a limiting mindset—one that is often the greatest obstacle to people in their individual efforts to bring about positive change. It's not the company that needs to change, it's the people within it. Think Talk Create is the toolkit at your disposal to articulate your values and fulfill your sense of purpose, positively impacting the culture of your organization along the way.

9

THE WILL TO BELIEVE

With Choice Comes Responsibility for Change

Every now and again, the voice in your head will challenge the belief that you are capable of changing your organization's culture or, more broadly, positively impacting the world around you. There will be a reluctance, a nervousness, to put Think Talk Create into practice. But in order to reshape the world, you must first believe yourself capable.

More than a century of cognitive research, the most rigorous of which has been conducted over the past couple of decades, has confirmed the powerful role played by how we think about ourselves. William James's notion of the "will to believe" is backed up by research on cognitive behavioral therapy (CBT), which reveals that the primary determinant of our feelings and behaviors is our underlying thoughts and beliefs. A broad range of mental health conditions, including anxiety and major depression, respond well to CBT, with a growing body of outcomes-based research confirming its effectiveness. Neuroimaging studies are attempting to elucidate the brain mechanisms for how CBT works and, by extension, for how we make choices about what to think and what to do.[1]

Neuroplasticity is the key characteristic of brain cells that empower growth and change in the frontal lobe and the amygdala, in addition to other regions of the limbic system. CBT, like active inquiry, serves an integrative function, as the human brain tries to deploy behaviors and thoughts in the service of health and adaptation. Active inquiry and CBT are both forms of dialogue that propel productive thinking, discussion, and social well-being.

It's critical to remember that our thoughts and beliefs don't just happen to us; we don't have to be passive recipients of them. In fact, as long as our minds are basically intact (without major psychiatric illness or dementia, for example), we can all be human beings who are free—and, in fact, morally responsible—to choose belief systems that help improve the lives of others and move the world forward in positive ways. There is a growing body of neuroimaging research revealing the potency of changes in brain functioning that are tied to CBT and to mindful self-reflection and intentional shifts in one's belief system.[2]

William James not only illuminated the power of believing in your own efficacy; he also exhorted us to put our choices and beliefs into action. Attempting to distance themselves from strictly theoretical and ossified philosophical

systems from Europe (epitomized by the works of philosophers like Immanuel Kant), James and his colleagues believed that truth resides only in the real, messy world of our
everyday lives, not in a universe of disembodied concepts.
As a result, they created our country's only fully homegrown
philosophy: American pragmatism. This school of thought
holds that ideas are developed in our minds to help us ma-
neuver across the landscape under our feet. As soon as we
choose, for example, to adopt the belief that dehumanization is harmful to our economy and our work culture, the
belief that we can institute positive work environments—
rooted in trust and psychological safety—comes within our
grasp. Then we each can commit to taking pragmatic action
to make it the new normal.

Voting with Your Feet

James's philosophy and experimental psychology, combined
with the neuroscience of cognitive therapy, came together in
the twentieth century to make possible Marianne Bertrand's
powerful speech to the University of Chicago class of 2018.
Agency is something Bertrand discussed in her convocation address, in a way, by demanding the recognition and
assumption of responsibility on the part of her audience. She
is not giving license to these graduates to pass the buck, so
to speak, and pin the shortfalls of poor corporate behavior
on the organization. You have the agency to enact change,
she said. It's one thing to want to work for a company with

values, as many of these new graduates do. And it's wonderful to know some organizations out there do, in fact, have a strong sense of purpose. But it's another thing to fall under a company's spell and blame the organization for exhibiting poor behavior, expecting it to change. In other words, don't waste time and energy either extolling or condemning the values of a company. Spend that effort figuring out what contribution, small or large, you might make to change it. That might, in some cases, entail striking out on your own as an entrepreneur to create a new organization or business.

Joe Morone and Diana Brazzell did just that. They are the cofounders of Footnote, a start-up that has become steadily profitable over the last several years. Joe and Diana recognized a major unmet need in the contemporary world: translating complex, evidence-based research into user-friendly, accessible language that could create an impact beyond strictly academic circles. They didn't see any other company or organization doing this well, so they made the choice to do it themselves.

Footnote describes itself as "an online media company that increases the impact of academic knowledge by making it accessible and engaging for new audiences." Its pragmatic mission of "showcasing research with the power to change the world" is carried out by partnering with professors and universities to transform technical research reports into articles published on widely read platforms, including leading magazines and newspapers.[3] This liberates valuable research that otherwise might get trapped in the quantitative purgatory of professional journals with a narrow readership and minimal real-world impact. It creates the possibility that new discoveries can have a positive effect on our everyday lives.

Joe and Diana (and members of their growing team) converse and collaborate closely with their clients, engaging in the Think Talk Create process with successful academics to enable their research to have a broader reach. Footnote's three key services of strategic communication, content creation, and publication and promotion provide the framework to drive these results. By asking open-ended questions about what the researchers' work is all about and why it matters, the Footnote team prompts these academics to expand their mindset about what they're up to. The scientists develop a wider perspective on their own work, and then they can collaborate with Joe, Diana, and the Footnote team to craft a publishable article that casts the work in a new and more widely influential light.

Footnote is also out front on the development of a positive workplace that fosters active inquiry through psychological safety and open discussion of core values. At a pivotal moment in the early development of the company, Joe and Diana employed active inquiry as they were struggling to generate enough revenue to stay afloat. Throughout their conversations, they kept asking themselves, "How much is this fulfilling us?" and "What do we really want Footnote to become?" The active inquiry process led them to make the choice to develop the company in a focused way and not get distracted by potential revenue-generating projects that weren't consistent with their core mission. They reassured one another about the positive outcomes that were likely to come as they deepened their commitment to why they had launched Footnote in the first place.

Footnote is increasingly profitable and has developed a sustainable business model rooted in active inquiry among the company's leadership group and in partnerships with the universities and researchers Footnote serves. The company's success is stunning. It has had successful engagements with more than two hundred academics from major institutions including Arizona State, Brown, Columbia, Harvard, Stanford, UC Berkeley, and the University of Southern California. Footnote's engaging, evidence-based articles have been published in media outlets including *Entrepreneur, Fortune, Harvard Business Review, Inside Higher Ed*, and the *Washington Post.*

Joe and Diana are successful entrepreneurs whose sense of agency and responsibility has led to an inspiring outcome. They have the kind of mindset that will be required to solve a plethora of worldwide problems, such as the environmental crisis. There is certainly a strong sense among an increasingly concerned public that something must be done to turn the tide of climate change. The government can levy carbon taxes on bad corporate actors and organizations can innovate new, sustainable energy solutions. But instead of simply pointing a finger at "them," we must also practice active inquiry with ourselves and those around us. We could expend more of our energy considering our own slice of responsibility: What can I do to enact positive environmental change?

For example, three of the top five steps recommended for curbing climate change are individual actions and behaviors: eating less meat, wasting less food, and better managing the use of coolants (air conditioners and common refrigerators).[4] So while we should support organizational efforts to install onshore wind turbines and restore tropical forests (the remaining two steps that round out the top five), we mustn't simply wait on the actions of "them." It's on us as individuals who make choices on behalf of companies and on behalf of ourselves to have a frank active inquiry session in the mirror. If we change as individuals, then companies will change, because—as our friend needed reminding that day—we are the companies.

Sometimes our position in relation to the size of the organization makes enacting change a bit more difficult. For example, it would be unfair to suggest that an Amazon factory worker can single-handedly change Amazon's quantitative culture. They certainly can take the small step of practicing active inquiry at work, building one psychologically safe relationship, then another, and another. As we know, these psychologically safe environments actually increase productivity and performance, so we hope it wouldn't be an effort that's met with any negativity by Amazon's distribution managers. There's no guarantee of that, just a reasonable hope that all the compelling research on trust and psychological safety will become part of more workplace discussions.

Still, if the cultivation of trust is for some reason chided by an organization's leadership, Bertrand—along with James—gives graduates the confidence to vote with their feet. Leaving one's job is not a luxury we all have, so while some can exit an organization if the culture proves unfixable, others will unfortunately have to stay put until they are in a better position to transition into a new outside role. But for these new graduates, voting with their feet is not necessarily leaving an unchangeable company; it can also mean, now that they're entering the job market, that they should proactively walk in the direction of companies that genuinely align with their desired sense of purpose and values. They can choose which set of glass doors they are going to walk through on Monday morning.

Voting with your feet is the same sentiment as voting with your dollars as a consumer. Not only do we have agency as employees, but we also have tremendous individual responsibility to enact positive change as consumers. The short-termism, metrics, and bottom-line thinking—the quantitative mindset—that exists within organizations around the world is not the company's mindset, after all. It's the perspective of the individuals that make up that company and the customers who purchase its goods and services.

When organizations do bad things—the behavior of large banks that fueled the 2008 financial crisis comes readily to mind—those at the top have a history of escaping personal consequences. Many people are working to change that tradition, with good cause. And yet the issue remains as to the responsibility of the hundreds of thousands of employees whose work can be, and often is, deployed toward carrying out deadly mistakes. For seventy-five years, the German people have wrestled with the responsibility of individual citizens in going along with the Nazi regime. But not everyone can risk life and livelihood, pick up their pitchfork, and storm the barricades at the first sign of trouble—and the longer one waits, the harder it is to take a stand. Even in the best case, the issue of a follower's responsibility makes for hard moral wrestling.

Her Name Is Samya

This dilemma was brought into sharp relief one cold, wet day in April 2019, outside Chicago's Field Museum. From a rain-soaked placard, the face of Samya Stumo stared out toward a cluster of blue-and-white umbrellas marked by the Boeing logo as investors lined up to enter the company's annual shareholders' meeting. Samya's uncle, Tarek Milleron, held up the placard with his niece's face. She had died on Ethiopian Airlines Flight 302, in a Boeing-made 737 Max 8 that nose-dived into the ground. The sad fact is that if anyone felt that she could make a difference through individual effort, it was Samya, who was a public-health advocate working in Africa to bring medical care to those who need it most.

For decades, Boeing had been the corporate epitome of pride and purpose in crafting gold-standard airplanes, where quality, safety, and maintenance were unquestioned. "If it's not Boeing, I'm not going!" was the watchword. Now those days seem to be a distant memory.

The 737 had been Boeing's iPhone, the product for which the company was best known and which filled the corporate bank accounts. But Boeing was feeling intense pressure from its chief competitor, the European company Airbus. The two firms were jockeying for first place in a constant battle over their commercial airline customers. When Airbus announced the launch of the A320neo—the A320 being the principal rival for the Boeing 737, both of which dominate the single-aisle airliner market—Boeing leaders' initial response was to be patient, take their time, and build an even better airplane. They knew they would lose market share in single-aisle planes for a couple of years, but a newer, faster, better, stronger airplane would bring their customers back.

But just a few months later, Boeing scrapped the brand-new aircraft idea in favor of a Band-Aid solution: a makeshift upgrade of the 737, dubbed the Max. Company executives had done the numbers and determined that a couple of years of lost sales of planes costing in the range of $100 million each was just too much to take.[5] Not only that, but the billions they'd be losing would wind up in the coffers of their stalwart competitor from across the pond.

When Boeing announced its decision to update the 737 with the Max line, its stock price soared. Orders came in for more than five thousand Max-type planes. Some airlines even built new routes into their schedules because of the anticipated benefits the Max 8 offered.[6] The 737 Max 8 was looking to replace the 737 as Boeing's cash cow, as industry experts estimated the aircraft would come to account for up to 40 percent of Boeing's annual profit.[7]

But in a shortsighted move meant to trim a few dollars off the price tag, Boeing decided to make some safety features optional rather than standard, which was a bit like making lifeboats optional on a cruise ship. Boeing's quantitative analysts had been tempted by their confreres at the airlines, often operating in cash-strapped developing countries, to play their own numbers game and bet on cost savings rather than passenger safety. To round out this catastrophe in the making, Boeing neglected to tell airlines and pilots about a possible software glitch that could make the 737 Max 8 take an uncontrollable nosedive.[8]

Boeing was following the teachings of modern scientific management and keeping its eyes on the numbers: the dates on a calendar for delivery of the aircraft, the dollars to be made or lost. In so doing, Boeing managers neglected the human element, and the human cost of the risk they were taking. Suspended were the old-school values that had always driven Boeing's profitability: pride, quality, precision, and an overriding concern for public safety. If any corporate initiative ever cried out for active inquiry, it was the 737 Max 8.

Like FMF Life, Boeing prioritized shareholder value over all else, but its shortsightedness didn't just make employees miserable and destroy careers. It led the company to put jets on the market that would kill hundreds of people. It turns out, though, that as much as Wall Street hates bad earnings reports, it hates it even more when an aircraft manufacturer neglects safety considerations and produces planes that fall out of the sky.

There are many ways for a company to blunder, and often these mistakes involve a simple lack of empathy, driven by an inflexible commitment to immediately hitting the numbers. But five months before the crash of Samya's flight in March 2019, Lion Air Flight 610 (also using a brand-new Boeing 737 Max 8) had plunged into the sea just after takeoff in Indonesia, killing all 189 onboard. Even after the first massive catastrophe, Boeing doubled down on its mistakes. A second crash resulted in more loss of life. The decline and death of a legendary company is not beyond the realm of possibility.

But "Boeing" didn't make that decision. The individual members of its leadership team did—those tasked with serving as stewards for the once-respected legacy brand. Had others been in those roles, there is a chance Boeing would not have embarked on the problematic Max journey. It's also perhaps the case that these individual executives did not believe themselves capable of making a course correction. Maybe they hadn't absorbed James's wisdom regarding the "will to believe." This is one of the most salient points in Marianne Bertrand's speech, but it is one that is so easy to overlook: Yes, you do have a choice. Yes, you can be an active agent for cultural change. But you must first believe yourself capable of bringing change about.

Samya was the niece of the pioneering consumer advocate Ralph Nader, who in 1965 had published *Unsafe at Any Speed: The Designed-In Dangers of the American Automobile*. Over half a century later, a beloved family member died as a result of corporate obsession with profits and neglect of the basic human concern for preserving life. Meanwhile, rather than benefiting from the unwavering focus on profits, Boeing's balance sheet suffered. By early 2020, orders and deliveries of Boeing aircraft fell to a sixteen-year low, with many orders going instead to rival Airbus.[9] Less than a year after the second fatal Boeing 737 Max 8 crash—the one that took Samya's life—Dennis Muilenburg, Boeing's CEO, was asked to resign. He received a golden parachute in excess of $60 million.[10] The 346 passengers on the Lion Air and Ethiopian Airlines flights had received no parachute at all.

The 737 Max 8 tragedy might have been averted if there had been a different work environment at Boeing, where employees and executives could have engaged in active inquiry and meaningful dialogue as to when it would be appropriate to bring the new aircraft to market. As it happened, the process was rushed and poorly regulated because of motivations for profit. An article in *Bloomberg* in December 2019 observed that "emphasis on the bottom line disrupted decades of productive communication between pilots, engineers, and designers."[11]

The company would have benefited from slowing the process down a bit, at least enough to promote structured dialogue among executives, engineers, other employees, and even board members and shareholders. There are many ways to structure these conversations, but they must be guided by curiosity and learning. They could have been framed around such open-ended questions as: What safety features should be standard on the 737 Max 8 before we sell and deliver it? How does this compare to what the financial analysts think? How do we balance shareholder drive for quick profit and other stakeholders' interests in safety? How could our reputation and long-term profits be affected by a worst-case scenario? It's hard to say for sure that more dialogue around these questions would have brought a different result, but there would have been no better way to create that possibility.

Boeing and other multibillion-dollar companies such as FedEx and UPS, whose problems with worker safety we recounted earlier, are capable of adopting new safety procedures and improving working conditions. But consider, too, why these organizations are so heavily focused on efficiency and delivery times, sometimes at the unfortunate expense of the health and safety of their teams. A premium is placed on speed because individual and corporate customers demand that packages be delivered on time, and one of UPS's biggest customers is Amazon.

FedEx claims that less than 1 percent of its annual revenue is tied to Amazon, and it works with other e-commerce giants like Walmart.[12] UPS, on the other hand, delivered nearly four hundred million packages for Amazon in 2018 alone, which some experts estimate to account for nearly 10 percent of UPS's annual revenue.[13] Therefore, the Amazon relationship is one on which UPS places a tremendous amount of value, for obvious monetary reasons. With Amazon offering its Prime customers free two-day shipping and even same-day shipping on some items in specific markets, we can understand the pressure UPS is under to ensure these deliveries are made correctly and on time.

So, to follow the quantitative chain of events: FedEx and UPS managers place incredible pressure on their delivery teams, often at the expense of driver well-being. The reason for the quantitative pressure, though, is because their customers demand efficiency and low shipping costs. Some of these customers include quantitatively oriented executives at giants like Walmart and Amazon, who command a massive share of the American e-commerce market. Fixated on their own bottom line, these companies have themselves struggled in recent years with reports of dehumanized environments for their employees. But costs must ultimately be kept to a minimum because their customers love to have a product delivered on the very same day it is ordered, or within forty-eight hours at the very least.

Amazon didn't offer—and keep—same-day shipping because it was an unpopular idea. The company is expanding it because individual customers love getting their $3 questionably manufactured socks within twenty-four hours. So the quantitative forces of dehumanization ultimately can be traced back to each of us as consumers. It is our desire for quick delivery and immediate gratification that props up the very economic system that is causing such massive stress, declines in quality of life, and untimely deaths.

Since the root of the problem can be traced back to us as individuals, we are confronted again with uncomfortable questions about personal responsibility and agency. We have many choices to make in our everyday lives, not least of which is the choice of how to think and what to believe. For example, a person may exercise their "will to believe" by deciding that the long-term health of the natural world is important to them, and that if they turn off their air conditioner, it will have a positive effect on the environment. It then requires the commitment to putting that idea into practice: yes, I can and will turn down my air conditioner. The confrontation of agency lies in our realization that there is, in fact, a problem in need of solving and we can influence the course of events through our well-considered decisions and actions.

Corporations and societies are made up of people just like us: some are the CEOs of publicly traded companies, and some are the buyers of unneeded items that certainly don't have to be delivered overnight. Regardless of who we are, the problems in our numbers-dominated culture can only be solved through a grassroots effort. The CEO, as an individual, may ask herself what she can do to show the shareholders that the greatest enhancement of value will be pro-social decisions to make the work environment more humane. She certainly would be able to draw on robust research findings suggesting that profits will likely rise over a reasonable course of time if trust, empathy, and psychological safety are in place. The sock purchaser and the person who leaves the air conditioner running on high, also as individuals, may similarly reflect upon the pros and cons of continuing to engage in behaviors that run contrary to some of their values.

Even before COVID-19 struck, before the Me Too movement and the Black Lives Matter movement, every organization faced vexing decisions about how to motivate and lead in our postindustrial, networked twenty-first century. No one can get away with ignoring the demand for growth and profitability. At the same time, we won't survive if we don't reverse the trend toward increasingly toxic work environments and create more humane settings, where people can actually think, talk, create, and thereby make more substantial contributions. We must transcend the exclusive focus on short-term earnings and look more carefully at how companies can ensure safety—whether psychological safety or aviation safety—so that their stock value and profitability don't go down in flames.

10

PROJECT SOCRATES

Making Active Inquiry a Way of Life

Think Talk Create is designed to promote human values and quality of life in a society that is largely underpinned by capitalism, science, and technology. We do not, it is crucial to point out, take issue with quantitative data, metrics, numbers, financial assessments, budget balancing, measurement, or growth. We're also not advocating in any way for a radical change, for capitalism itself to be repealed and replaced by a new system. The principles of capitalism, in fact, carry tremendous potential in their ability to positively transform the world. Capitalism is arguably the most constructive economic force known to humanity, a system that has alleviated poverty, cured disease, and instilled global peace. But, as a human system, capitalism is equally capable of egregious acts of inhumanity. We're merely advocating for a straightforward but powerful change, a mindset shift that can be cultivated through the inherently human process of dialogue.

"We know what we are, but know not what we may be," says Ophelia in Shakespeare's *Hamlet*.[1] Even if we know what we are at this moment, we can still attempt to influence the unknown and do more than hope for what may be. Although it is within the realm of the future, what we may be—our collective potential—can only be determined by our individual actions. What we become is determined by our choices and the pragmatic steps we take to realize them.

The Hallmark of Humanity

With the deceptively simple process of active inquiry, we can each do our bit to meet the challenges of our day: from climate change to product and worker safety and beyond. The structured process of humanistic change—Think Talk Create—hinges on our acknowledgement and ownership of choice and of agency. The choice may be the unornamented action of asking an open-ended question to those who populate our lives, such as an unassuming elderly customer entering the store of a billion-dollar company or a colleague nearing the end of his rope. Behind every statistic and metric and algorithm and balance sheet stands a human soul whose dignity hinges on our setting aside the raft of numbers, at least for a few moments, and really listening.

Active inquiry has moral and ethical value. Asking open-ended questions nonjudgmentally conveys respect and ensures dignity in conversational exchanges. It is a valuable thing in itself, independent of its pragmatic and monetary benefits for companies. It's worth teaching not only to adults, but also to children and adolescents who are engaged in the prolonged process of brain and personality development. A full embrace of active inquiry in educational and business settings may constitute the most powerful force we can muster against dehumanization. That is good for everyone, including employees, bosses, executives, shareholders, and every other person who interacts with these individuals.

Conceptualizing active inquiry as a moral imperative adds to its potency in personal and business settings. When we engage intentionally in active inquiry and respectfully listen to people, we reduce their stress, buttress their self-worth, and reinforce their basic humanity. It allows us to create positive workplaces and propel societal stability and growth. We should think of active inquiry as more than just a set of techniques to ensure productive conversations and profitable corporations.

Seemingly small conversational shifts can have exponential benefits across entire human societies. It can serve as the engine of widespread culture change, allowing biologically and psychologically flawed humans to create communities that thrive and grow. It's our best bet to reduce the partisanship and polarization that each year seems to get worse in American politics. If only those in positions of influence would take some time to learn and master active inquiry, and then apply it in the halls of power for the good of all.

Young people, most notably millennials and Generation Z, are attentive to the importance of companies contributing not just to the bottom line and the interests of shareholders, but also to society more broadly. Companies that don't take a moral stance on key topics of the day, such as social justice and environmental protections, are at risk of receiving negative media attention and struggling to attract and retain top-tier employees. This younger generation is insisting on strategies like active inquiry and Think Talk Create to fuel conversations about how companies can do good as much as they do well.

Active inquiry can empower the development of capitalism with a conscience. Bringing respect, dignity, and moral values to work should be the pinnacle of any economic system that has some sense of purpose other than raw survival. Active inquiry promotes collaboration, brainstorming, and profitability. Just because it focuses on enhancing the quality of social relations among people spanning the entire socioeconomic spectrum doesn't mean that utilizing active inquiry and treating people with respect amounts to any form of political or economic "socialism." The empirical research demonstrates that business teams that promote trust, collaboration, and respect for divergent ideas are the ones with the highest levels of performance and profitability.

Active inquiry has intrinsic benefits even before we get to dollars and cents. A 2018 research article published in the journal *Psychological Science* reported on the remarkable effects in the brain of talking with children rather than to or at them.[2] That distinction is at the core of active inquiry. Conversational exchanges with children of all ages, akin to the active inquiry process with fully developed adults, results in observable activity in the regions of the brain (including Broca's area) that are responsible for language processing. Novel neuroimaging research is providing remarkable evidence of this phenomenon. This brain activation also predicts scores on language assessments.[3] The potency of active inquiry comes into play decades before adults show up in the workplace. Parents and teachers are the first bosses or managers that we encounter in our lifetimes. That's why early experiences with active inquiry can enhance later success in social situations and in our careers.

As such, active inquiry is both conceptually and pragmatically transformational, but it can be developed and strengthened only with attention and practice. It draws on all of our cognitive and social assets that have been the gift of evolution—yet it is distinctly human, our highest good. We alone have the capacity to proactively engage in dialogues guided by open-ended questions, careful listening, and conversations that result in group self-preservation, as well as innovation, creativity, and productivity.

Think Talk Create can move the twenty-first-century world in a direction that will improve our politics and allow for global cooperation to protect the environment. It can help to give billions of people the opportunity for safety, comfort, and thriving. That's how big we can go with it. Think Talk Create can and should be our newest evolutionary adaptation in this technical, quantitative, and increasingly dehumanized age. From everyday interactions with family members and coworkers to discussions in the halls of global political power, human success relies more than ever on a thoroughgoing adoption of active inquiry.

After all, the primary step in the active inquiry process is to take a mindful pause to identify your internal belief system: to think. Given that our underlying cognitions about who we are in the world largely determine how we act, we need a clear handle on them. This belief system is the driver of the questions we ask. Without self-awareness, asking a relevant and thought-provoking open-ended question is an impossibility. Which takes us back once more to the ancient Greeks and the admonition from the Temple of Apollo at Delphi: know thyself. The most important person you can use active inquiry with is looking back at you in the mirror each morning.

It's a hallmark of humanity that we can engage in the process of deep self-reflection, asking ourselves tough questions without already having a preconceived answer. This process has a proud tradition in philosophy and an emerging basis in modern-day neuroimaging. In Western philosophy, the tradition extends most notably back to Saint Augustine who, in his *Confessions* (written in the late fourth century AD), reflected on his youthful sins and delineates his conversion to Christianity. Centuries later in *Meditations on First Philosophy*, René Descartes looked inward in search of a foundational thought that must be true (and not the deceptions of an "evil demon"). Rigorously rejecting a long line of potential true beliefs, he settled on what would become a defining phrase of Western philosophy: "Cogito, ergo sum" (I think, therefore I am).

In the modern era of neuroscience, the study of self-reflection has largely moved away from monasteries and ivory towers and into the MRI suite in hospitals and research centers. A functional MRI (fMRI) of the brain is capable of delineating regions with heightened metabolic activity during various mental tasks. When human subjects in these experiments engage in self-reflective tasks, fMRI reliably shows activation in both the limbic system and the frontal cortex. In a 2012 research paper published by *BMC Neuroscience*, the authors described the study intervention: "A short, exclusively mental process of self-reflection in the absence of external stimuli or behavioral requirements."[4] The task resulted in significant "dorsomedial and lateral prefrontal, insular, anterior and posterior cingulate" activations. These are the areas that underlie Daniel Kahneman's system 1 (the cingulate cortex of the limbic system) and system 2 (the frontal lobe). Since active inquiry involves a careful combination of emotional relatedness to others and rational analysis, it serves as the integrator of systems 1 and 2. Whether we are asking ourselves a good question or inquiring into the mind of another person, self-reflection is an absolute necessity. These fMRI studies reveal a likely neural substrate for active inquiry, thereby lending it even more credence in our evidence-based world.

The inward process of Think Talk Create—the self-reflective capacity to ask thought-provoking and open-ended questions—is the basis on which to engage in active inquiry with someone else. If you can't regulate your emotions and cognitive processes well enough to formulate good questions in your own mind, how can you ever do that with another person? Conversely, our internal development of strong questions can be shaped by the responses and contributions of our conversation partners. Active inquiry directed toward oneself and toward others are two sides of the same coin.

As we write this book, American society is going through a reckoning about how we balance public health and economic activity. Our explorations in this book have woven between the worlds of health care and business. The COVID-19 pandemic has put the two on a collision course unlike anything we've seen in our lifetimes. Much of it amounts to a consideration of quantitative and humanistic reasoning. Many political and business leaders railed against lockdowns to prevent the spread of the coronavirus because of concerns about job losses and economic decline. They made the important point that such a scenario puts people's physical and mental health at risk. Opening up the economy quickly could bring short-term economic stability but would risk further worsening of the pandemic and more business shutdowns later. The humanistic focus of shutting down parts of the economy quickly, in order to spare people severe illness and death caused by COVID-19, could have a positive long-term economic benefit as restrictions get reduced in the future, when the virus is contained.

In times like this, people need a frontal lobe that can absorb the emotions (such as fear and anger) emanating from the limbic system and transform them into careful reflections on what's safe, valuable, and meaningful. As the story of Phineas Gage showed, the frontal lobe serves as the chief executive of the brain. It allows us to regulate our emotions, make plans, and take well-sequenced actions in the service of a salient goal. We each need a high-functioning frontal lobe to run our lives well. And as a society, we need our leaders to serve as our metaphorical frontal lobe, deliberately and wisely guiding us toward decisions consistent with our values. When this is going smoothly, we can witness the Think Talk Create process at work. Lately, though, that's not been the case as much as we'd like. For some businesses and governments in the early stages of the 2020s, things have not gotten off to an ideal start. At times, our society has looked as impaired and dysfunctional as Phineas Gage in the aftermath of his traumatic brain injury.

The pandemic of 2020 brought the tension between health and economics to a boiling point. The economic slowdown, with tens of millions of people out of work, created a tinderbox of fear and anger across the United States and in many other parts of the world. The brutal police killing of George Floyd in the spring, along with the ensuing protests and riots, further threw society into disequilibrium. A rancorous and inflammatory run-up to the 2020 US presidential election, and what ensued in its aftermath, only created more jitters. Eventually, we can hope, this kind of unrest may lead to positive movements toward greater social and economic equality.

What we need is open dialogue about how to balance the exigencies of public health and maintaining enough economic activity so that a recession or depression wouldn't create more devastation than the coronavirus was already doing. In some nations, where government institutions have been on a sounder footing, temporary shutdowns allowed them to quell the virus. Governments made adequate provisions to help people who were most harmed by the abrupt and extreme changes. Things were much more haphazard and poorly planned in the United States.

In the midst of these epic failures of broad-ranging societal leadership, many individuals and companies stepped up to the plate and provided the frontal lobe that the government didn't appear to have. A national consulting firm with whom we work provided a firsthand view of how to handle a public health and economic crisis with equanimity, respect, and an eye to long-term growth and profitability.

As its employees suddenly needed to transition to working from home, the company's leadership communicated proactively and often. The CEO and managers across multiple disciplines immediately began asking questions—by email, phone, or video conference—about how people were doing and what they needed to work effectively and comfortably from home. Managers didn't monitor whether employees were logged in to the company's computer system and doing company work throughout the day. Instead, they encouraged employees to take all the breaks they needed, attend to children and pets, and focus more on work results than processes. In other words, they treated their employees like adults and fostered a psychologically safe culture, genuinely seeking any and all feedback about how the company could adapt to the new realities. The employees were offered weekly wellness and mindfulness sessions. Throughout the pandemic, the company continually asked how people felt about continuing to work from home even after the governor would allow offices to reopen. There was a wide range of responses, and the company decided to take a flexible approach to office- and home-based work indefinitely. Some people missed the interactions on-site, while others were thrilled not to commute and found themselves more productive in the absence of office distractions. Each person would have the opportunity to choose how to work in the future.

The consulting firm took a similar approach to its customers in various regions of the United States. Despite a downturn in new business opportunities as the pandemic set in, the company offered its clients online resiliency seminars and workshops at a reduced cost or for free. They trusted that maintaining the quality of the relationship while adding value during a crisis would eventually pay off. The firm maintained reality-based hope and confidence for the future. There were no layoffs and few people were furloughed.

Outside contractors received less work, but the company bolstered relationships with them by way of seminars and conference calls to field questions and facilitate discussion.

Despite at least 30 percent less monthly revenue than projected for 2020, leaders and employees across the company thought it was a highly successful year. By strengthening its relationships and engaging in active inquiry in many forms, the company built trust with its employees and customers. The low revenue numbers and razor-thin profit margins were concerning but overshadowed by the human handling of the crisis. This company was built for the future. Even in the midst of a completely novel public health disaster, company leadership kept its cool and sidestepped a treacherous fall into purely quantitative thinking.

People and companies that succeed both quantitatively and in human terms, we have seen, place high value on active inquiry, psychological safety, and empathy. They avoid dehumanization by respecting people's dignity and fostering an environment rooted in trust and collaboration. They empower people to function in a calm brain state, free of amygdala hijack, with their frontal lobes—where emotion and reason are integrated—guiding strong decision-making based on both numbers and moral sentiments. Weaving all of these approaches together is essential, but not easy or straightforward.

The COVID-19 pandemic brought this dynamic into high relief, with some companies clamping down further on rigid metrics to try to ride out the storm. Fortunately, others took a longer view of the situation, trying to retain good workers by keeping them on the payroll and paying them as much of their usual salary as possible.

The flawed response of the US government to the COVID-19 crisis underscores the point. By opening the economy too quickly in the hope of preserving favorable economic numbers in the short term, some US states fed further coronavirus outbreaks that led not only to more deaths and more cases of serious illness but to more serious shutdowns only a month or two later, resulting in a much larger financial hit and further rounds of job losses.

The pandemic was the quintessential case of a dilemma tailor-made for active inquiry. COVID-19 presented an incredibly complex problem that could be solved only by drawing on expertise from many different fields in order to balance two compelling but competing interests: maintaining a healthy economy and maintaining the health of the nation. But instead of engaging in open-ended conversations where all voices were heard and nothing was off-limits, the Trump administration immediately began trying to play the crisis for partisan advantage, or at least limit the pandemic's ability to damage the administration's narrative of "making America great again." Expert opinion was dismissed out of hand, and crackpot ideas (drinking bleach?!) were floated without careful consideration. Stock prices and GDP numbers took precedence over the number of human fatalities. Above all, the US response reflected a go-it-alone attitude and a distrust of collective action, both on the part of the administration vis-à-vis other nations, and within the United States on the part of those who, insisting that the crisis was overblown, refused to wear masks, socially isolate, or otherwise follow precautions.

How a massive public health crisis turned into a strident political battle is, without question, a complex and disturbing matter. But one thing is clear: active inquiry was almost nowhere to be found, certainly not in the nation's capital. Where were the open-minded, civil conversations among leaders with different perspectives about how we might protect each other's health and promote economic well-being at the same time? There was no office for Socrates in the West Wing.

Math Ends, Philosophy Begins

Throughout the pandemic, we were flooded with an endless, daily stream of numbers and statistics: new coronavirus cases, test positivity rates, hospitalizations, deaths. Alongside the coronavirus numbers, we were constantly informed of unemployment numbers, the value of the S&P 500, and congressional bickering over economic relief. Rather than gorging on even more numbers, Socrates certainly would've posed bigger-picture questions about how we balance our values and direct our efforts. We all have the agency to ask these questions in our own lives and workplaces; there's simply no justification for expecting answers about how to conduct ourselves to come from the government or any authority beyond ourselves and our communities.

Even before Socrates, there was a group of thinkers (conveniently known as the pre-Socratics) who were concerned with fundamental questions such as: "What is this world we live in?" and "What is its defining force?" (questions, mind you, that still remain unanswered over 2,500 years later). One of the pre-Socratics, named Thales, thought the earth had an origin story and that its core defining force was a tangible and measurable thing within it: water. His friend, Anaximander, agreed that the earth had an origin story, but he argued that its defining force was instead an immeasurable, infinite thing, the term for which he derived literally from the Greek for "without limits." Fast-forward a couple hundred years, and the rift between measurable and immeasurable remained.

When Socrates came along, he didn't write anything down because he said face-to-face conversation allowed for less misinterpretation. Fortunately, one of his primary followers was Plato. He was like the A student in class taking diligent notes, which he turned into his famous dialogues, many of which feature Socrates asking his timeless questions.

Plato then taught yet another famous philosopher, Aristotle, whom you could call Socrates's academic grandson. Plato and Aristotle didn't see eye to eye on everything. When the Italian artist Raphael painted his masterpiece *The School of Athens* around 1510, he featured Plato and Aristotle as central figures, placing them directly in the center of the fresco. Their union at the center of the painting also highlights the disunion at the core of their thinking. Plato's hand points up, toward the heavens, as he believed our world did not consist of measurable absolutes. Aristotle, in contrast, is painted with his hand stretched outward, parallel to the ground beneath him, as he believed items in the world consist of measurable properties. The painting evokes the tension we still experience between evidence-based science and philosophical consideration of our highest human values. At least Plato and Aristotle, as Raphael represented them, are talking to each other.

This tension is also palpable in the work of sixth-century-BC Greek scholar Pythagoras, whose theorem we all know from middle-school math class. The mathematical order of the universe elegantly manifests itself in his simple equation for relating the lengths of the sides of a triangle: the square of the hypotenuse (the side opposite the right angle) is always equal to the sum of the squares of the other two sides (famously written as $a^2 + b^2 = c^2$). This clarity about how numbers reflect nature carried across the centuries, culminating in Isaac Newton's three physical laws that constitute classical mechanics—including the equation $f = ma$, which denotes the fixed mathematical relations among any object's force, mass, and acceleration.

Importantly, though, Pythagoras also realized that the theory of rational numbers undermines itself, revealing forces that always disrupt any oversimplified quantitative science. He discovered that some numbers are not whole numbers—that is, not usable in simple fractions and equations. He called these irrational numbers, remarkable for their decimal expansions that never terminate. They continue to infinity, in no regular or predictable pattern (pi is probably the most well-known and useful of the irrational numbers). This is the ancient Greek foreshadowing of quantum mechanics and the higher-order displacement of Newton.

The idea of irrational numbers also captures the uncertainty of what a post-stroke patient with abulia might say in novel circumstances, which is not predictable by the laws of neuroscience. And it evokes the "irrational" numbers of modern-day behavioral economics, where people's spending decisions cannot be explained or predicted on the basis of their rational self-interest. The possibilities of how human beings will behave run toward infinity, like any good Pythagorean irrational number. From the vantage point of ancient Greece in the sixth century BC, Pythagoras had anticipated the findings of twenty-first-century scientists.

It's an ongoing question: What is the appropriate time and place for adopting a numerical mindset, in contrast to one that accounts for feelings, values, and other less-than-quantifiable things? It's a tension that existed between two ancient Greek thinkers, between two images portrayed by a Renaissance painter, between the godfather of twentieth-century neurology and his patient, and between businesses eager to meet their quarterly targets and the human employees who must ensure those targets are met.

One time in graduate school, we stopped by a well-known and well-traveled, but not well-dusted, bookshop just off the University of Chicago campus. While we browsed and purchased a considerable number of books from that shop—books full of paragraphs and ideas that shaped the world—it was an unknowing, anonymous employee who penned the most profound phrase we encountered as a result of searching its shelves.

Though bittersweet, the time had come for the store to move to a bigger, more modern space. But despite the store employees' best efforts to complete the move—from a dimly lit series of alcoves to endless rows of bright, sleek shelves—on time, they were running behind schedule. Students had returned to Chicago from the warmth of summer, classes were underway, reading lists were circulated, and yet the books in this new space were still not fully unpacked. A veritable scene of chaos and commotion persisted for those first few weeks of the semester, with students rifling through what appeared to be contemporary sculptures made out of brown cardboard boxes, all containing alphabetized, usually subject-specific texts.

In an effort to make some sense of the chaos, a store clerk created temporary signs, crudely printed on recycled paper, indicating the specific start and end point for each subject. Rows followed in alphabetical order from anthropology all the way to zoology. There, halfway down the procession of new shelves, as if painted by a modern-day Raphael, was a sign that simply read: "Mathematics Ends, Philosophy Begins."

That bookstore clerk was onto something. As we've argued throughout this book, too many organizations these days structure their decision-making around purely quantitative metrics. It is as though organizations have taken the guidance of the bookstore clerk and reversed it, pitting mathematics against philosophy: "Philosophy ends, and mathematics begins."

Numbers are critically important, and the empirical sciences have improved our lives in countless ways. We're by no means suggesting that mathematics should end. Quantitative data and analysis have helped us explore other planets, develop medicines for previously incurable diseases, and build powerful computer systems that are smaller than a matchbox. Numbers help companies measure financial performance, tell a story for prospective investors, and provide essential context when company leadership must make critical decisions. In other words, numbers are essential for running a business or a medical practice or almost any other modern-day profession. But organizations shouldn't rely on numbers alone. Research in favor of empathy and against dehumanization makes that clear. Research on psychological safety and behavioral economics reinforces the importance of enhancing the humanistic focus in workplaces if capitalism is to succeed in the future. Our Think Talk Create model draws all of these humanistic approaches together, integrating numbers and emotions into a workable methodology to achieve this goal.

Think Talk Create is an essential component of any professional career. That's because organizations need both mathematics and philosophy, not one or the other exclusively. Perhaps the genius behind Raphael's portrayal is that both Plato and Aristotle are represented in the center of the painting on equal footing. When it comes to the history of ideas, we should each learn from their collective example and use both hands, not one alone.

Numbers undoubtedly matter, and having a quantitative mindset is essential at the right times. But the humanistic side of things has gotten squeezed out of the picture as of late. The truth is that we often place insufficient value on profound emotions, nuances, social considerations, and other humanistic elements. Leaders, for example, talk about big-picture thinking without realizing what "big-picture" actually means. We're so focused on the numbers that we miss some pretty critical nonquantitative aspects of professional life. We miss what lurks behind the numbers and what is often the powerful determining force of success or failure.

Part of the issue is that we often conflate the two worlds, depicting quantitative methodologies in humanistic, even philosophical terms to make ourselves feel like we're covering both bases. After all, Google's hyper-quantitative workplace study was named Project Aristotle. There's even an artificial intelligence service that communicates with employees through a bot named Socrates. Having a bot named Socrates is a bit like having a player piano named Beethoven. It's a clever name, but it's a misnomer at the very least. We don't need a bot named Socrates in the workplace. What we need in the workplace is Socrates. What we need is Think Talk Create.

Acknowledgments

It's remarkable how tiny, seemingly insignificant acts can have life-changing effects on the people around you. We know this to be true because of our dear friend: writer, statesman, and all-around superb person Robert Bruce Rackleff. One day in early 2015, Bob cut out and mailed one of us an article from *The Economist* on how to bring philosophy into the business world. It set off a series of events that led to our meeting each other—soon-to-be collaborators, friends, and coauthors of this book—for the first time, in a café just outside Boston. The article, framed with Bob's accompanying note, hangs in our company's office to this day.

We are fortunate to have a great many people in our lives who, over a long period of time, listened and listened yet again to our ideas and aspirations. These include our parents—Jane and the late Robert Brendel, Donna and Paul Stelzer—and so many other members of our respective families: Git, Gary, Michael, John (not for reading drafts but for the ice cream), Lisa, Anthony, Nicholas, Barbara, Joe, Mary, Peggy, Mark, Thomas, Iruña, Gis-Xi, Carlos, Gia, Matt, Gustavo, Sabrina, Arianna, Max, Luke, Mary, Brian, and Joseph.

Thanks as well to Becca, to Isaac for his enthusiasm and careful attention to Chapter 7, and to Elias for his constructive commentary. And to Kelsey, and to Harry, and to the wisdom that exists beyond words.

We also thank close friends and colleagues for their support and valuable insights: Dan Brickman, Lauren Ortosky, Jamie Radice, Paul and Carolyn Cacolice, Cristina Corser, Julie Copoulos, Ian Reed, Sofie Suter, Matt DeLuca, Amanda Garcia, Teresa Reske, Carolyn and Kevin Schopp, Stephen and Fiona Roche, Rainer Rios, Sarah Tatgenhorst, Ryan Knapp, Christian Knapp, Connor Koziol, Lina Duarte, Daniel Riggs, Devin O'Brien, Dave Spallina, Greg Lynch, Shalin Desai, Claas Kirchhelle, Shanti Jones, Alex Gold, Eron Cohen, Stefan Kalt, Emmie Stamell, Karen Marinella Hall, Alex Vuckovic, Patrick McLaren, Andrew Neitlich, Stu Koman, Jim Greenblatt, Paula Vass, Bob Keane, Alec Bodkin, Melinda Merino, Gary Riccio, so many great colleagues at Keystone Partners, and, regrettably, Brian Farkas.

We've been fortunate to enjoy the company of some wonderful teachers and mentors over the years, and while it would be impossible to list them all here, we would like to especially acknowledge Fred Hochberg, Cathy Dillard, Carrie Wibben, Jim Cruse, Ravi Arulanantham, Keith Linhart, Ralph Lerner, C. Allen Speight, Gary Dineen, Jill Keenan,

Mary Hurley, Jeffrey Pettis, Lou Marinoff, Maurice Natanson, and Thomas Mann's unforgettable Hans Castorp of *The Magic Mountain*.

We extend heartfelt gratitude to the family of Samya Stumo, especially her mother, Nadia Milleron, uncle Tarek Milleron, and friend Mike Snavely. Their strength and courage are nothing short of incredible. It is a privilege and honor for us to tell Samya's story.

For the sake of privacy, we have changed the names of certain people featured in narratives throughout the book. In some cases, we've altered various details of the stories to further disguise people's identities. In all cases, we've preserved and highlighted the main points.

We thank the many scientists, academics, and researchers who were willing to share their insights with us, especially Elizabeth Necka, Rachel Romeo, Sandra Comas, Paul Zak, Marianne Bertrand, and William Belanger. The same goes for other innovators and influencers we spoke with, including Ralph Nader, the late John Bogle, Matthew Yglesias, and Douglas MacMillan.

The professionalism and wisdom of our editor, the incomparable John Mahaney, are unfathomable. We thank him for believing in this project and supporting us each step of the way. We extend our thanks as well to the entire team at PublicAffairs and Hachette, with special appreciation for Kelly Lenkevich and Liz Dana.

Lastly, we would like to thank the team at Kneerim & Williams in Boston, especially our marvelous agent, Carolyn

Savarese, whose constant encouragement and guidance made this book possible. A special thank-you is also due to Carolyn's partner in crime, William Patrick, who brilliantly helped us to develop our ideas from the early stages.

We believe in the Think Talk Create process because we have seen and lived it. We hope it inspires you as well.

Notes

Introduction: Counting Your Chickens Won't Make Them Hatch

1. Muir, William M., and David Sloan Wilson. "When the Strong Outbreed the Weak: An Interview with William Muir." *The Evolution Institute*, 11 July 2016, evolution-institute.org/when-the-strong-outbreed-the-weak-an-interview-with-william-muir/.
2. "One Million Species to Go Extinct 'Within Decades.'" Al Jazeera, 6 May 2019, www.aljazeera.com/news/2019/05/06/one-million-species-to-go-extinct-within-decades/.
3. Alexander, Amir. "Disorder Rules the Universe." *New York Times*, 16 Feb. 2015, www.nytimes.com/2015/02/17/science/the-quantum-moment-recounts-the-end-of-determinism.html.
4. Rostand, Jean. *Pensées d'un biologiste*. Paris: Stock, 1939.
5. Kahn, William A. "Psychological Conditions of Personal Engagement and Disengagement at Work." *Academy of Management Journal*, vol. 33, no. 4, 1990, pp. 692–724, doi:10.5465/256287.
6. Nickisch, Curt, and Amy Edmondson. "Creating Psychological Safety in the Workplace." *Harvard Business Review*, 22 Jan. 2020,

hbr.org/podcast/2019/01/creating-psychological-safety-in-the
-workplace.

7. Thompson, Leigh. "Go Ahead and Tell Your Most Embarrassing
   Story. It Will Boost Your Creativity." *Fast Company*, 19 Sept.
   2019, www.fastcompany.com/90406432/go-ahead-and-tell
   -your-most-embarrassing-story-it-will-boost-your-creativity.

8. Lublin, Joann S. "Companies Try a New Strategy: Empathy
   Training." *Wall Street Journal*, 21 June 2016, www.wsj.com
   /articles/companies-try-a-new-strategy-empathy-1466501403.

9. Wilson, Ernest J., III. "Empathy Is Still Lacking in the Leaders
   Who Need It Most." *Harvard Business Review*, 21 Sept. 2015,
   hbr.org/2015/09/empathy-is-still-lacking-in-the-leaders-who
   -need-it-most.

10. Jensen, Keld. "Intelligence Is Overrated: What You Really
    Need to Succeed." *Forbes*, 13 Nov. 2012, www.forbes.com
    /sites/keldjensen/2012/04/12/intelligence-is-overrated-what
    -you-really-need-to-succeed.

11. Williams, Ray. "The Biggest Predictor of Career Success? Not
    Skills or Education—but Emotional Intelligence." *Financial Post*,
    1 Jan. 2014, https://financialpost.com/executive/careers/the
    -biggest-predictor-of-career-success-not-skills-or-education
    -but-emotional-intelligence.

12. Swisher, Kara. "Who Will Teach Silicon Valley to Be Ethical?"
    New York Times, 21 Oct. 2018, www.nytimes.com/2018/10/21
    /opinion/who-will-teach-silicon-valley-to-be-ethical.html.

13. Walsh, Dylan. "The Workplace Is Killing People and Nobody
    Cares." *Insights by Stanford Business*, 15 Mar. 2018, www.gsb
    .stanford.edu/insights/workplace-killing-people-nobody-cares.

14. Virtanen, Marianna, et al. "Job Strain and Psychologic
    Distress." *American Journal of Preventive Medicine*, vol. 33, no.
    3, 2007, pp. 182–187, doi:10.1016/j.amepre.2007.05.003.

15. Krugman, Paul. "On the Economics of Not Dying." *New York
    Times*, 28 May 2020, www.nytimes.com/2020/05/28/opinion
    /coronavirus-economy-death.html.

Chapter 1: The Human Variable

1. Plato. *Plato: Five Dialogues*. Edited by John M. Cooper. Indianapolis, IN: Hackett, 2002.

Chapter 2: Building a Culture of Think Talk Create

1. Google. "Re:Work." 2015, rework.withgoogle.com/print/guides /5721312655835136/.
2. Duhigg, Charles. "What Google Learned from Its Quest to Build the Perfect Team." *New York Times*, 25 Feb. 2016, www .nytimes.com/2016/02/28/magazine/what-google-learned -from-its-quest-to-build-the-perfect-team.html.
3. Google. "Define 'Effectiveness.'" In *Guide: Understand Team Effectiveness*. Re:Work, 2015, rework.withgoogle.com/guides /understanding-team-effectiveness/steps/define-effectiveness/.
4. Google. "Define 'Effectiveness.'" In *Guide: Understand Team Effectiveness*. Re:Work, 2015, rework.withgoogle.com/guides /understanding-team-effectiveness/steps/define-effectiveness/.
5. Duhigg, Charles. "What Google Learned from Its Quest to Build the Perfect Team." *New York Times*, 25 Feb. 2016, www .nytimes.com/2016/02/28/magazine/what-google-learned -from-its-quest-to-build-the-perfect-team.html.
6. Ross, Judith A. "Make Your Good Team Great." *Harvard Business Review*, 7 Aug. 2014, hbr.org/2008/02/make-your-good-team -great-1.
7. Google. "Define 'Effectiveness.'" In *Guide: Understand Team Effectiveness*. Re:Work, 2015, rework.withgoogle.com/guides /understanding-team-effectiveness/steps/define-effectiveness/.
8. Kahn, William A. "Psychological Conditions of Personal Engagement and Disengagement at Work." Academy of Management Journal, vol. 33, no. 4, 1990, pp. 692–724, doi:10.5465/256287.
9. Herway, Jake. "How to Create a Culture of Psychological Safety." Gallup, 7 Dec. 2017, www.gallup.com/workplace/236198/create -culture-psychological-safety.aspx.

10. Google. "Identify Dynamics of Effective Teams." In *Guide: Understand Team Effectiveness*. Re:Work, 2015, rework.with google.com/guides/understanding-team-effectiveness/step s/identify-dynamics-of-effective-teams/.

11. Zak, Paul J. *Trust Factor: The Science of Creating High-Performance Companies*. New York: AMACOM, 2017.

12. Conger, Kate, and Daisuke Wakabayashi. "Google Fires 4 Workers Active in Labor Organizing." *New York Times*, 25 Nov. 2019, www.nytimes.com/2019/11/25/technology/google -fires-workers.html.

13. Bergen, Mark. "Google Workers Protest Company's 'Brute Force Intimidation.'" *Bloomberg*, 22 Nov. 2019, www.bloomberg .com/news/articles/2019-11-22/google-workers-protest -company-s-brute-force-intimidation.

14. Duhigg, Charles. "What Google Learned from Its Quest to Build the Perfect Team." *New York Times*, 25 Feb. 2016, www .nytimes.com/2016/02/28/magazine/what-google-learned -from-its-quest-to-build-the-perfect-team.html.

Chapter 3: Insufficient Evidence

1. Castro, D. R., et al. "Mere Listening Effect on Creativity and the Mediating Role of Psychological Safety." *Psychology of Aesthetics, Creativity, and the Arts*, vol. 12, no. 4, 2008, pp. 489– 502, doi:10.1037/aca0000177.

2. Freud, Sigmund. *New Introductory Lectures on Psycho-Analysis*. Edited by James Strachey. New York: W. W. Norton, 1990.

Chapter 4: Blinded by Being Right

1. Burke, Kenneth. *Permanence and Change: An Anatomy of Purpose*. Berkeley: University of California Press, 1984.

2. Canales, Katie. "Amazon CEO Jeff Bezos Said Social Media Is a 'Nuance-Destruction Machine' When Asked About His Views on 'Cancel Culture.'" *Business Insider*, 29 July 2020,

www.businessinsider.com/jeff-bezos-amazon-nuance
-destruction-machine-social-media-2020-7.

3. Twomey, Steve. "Phineas Gage: Neuroscience's Most Famous
Patient." *Smithsonian Institution*, Jan. 2010, www.smithsonianmag
.com/history/phineas-gage-neurosciences-most-famous
-patient-11390067/.

4. Kahneman, Daniel. *Thinking, Fast and Slow*. New York: Farrar,
Straus and Giroux, 2011.

5. Plato. *Phaedrus*. Translated by Robin Waterfield. Oxford:
Oxford University Press, 2009.

6. World Health Organization. "Burn-Out an 'Occupational
Phenomenon': International Classification of Diseases." 28 May
2019, www.who.int/mental_health/evidence/burn-out/en/.

7. Curtin, Sally C., Margaret Warner, and Holly Hedegaard.
"Increase in Suicide in the United States, 1999–2014." NCHS Data
Brief no. 241, 2016, https://pubmed.ncbi.nlm.nih.gov/27111185/.

8. National Institute of Mental Health. "Suicide." Sept. 2020,
www.nimh.nih.gov/health/statistics/suicide.shtml.

9. Case, Anne, and Angus Deaton. *Deaths of Despair and the Future
of Capitalism*. Princeton, NJ: Princeton University Press, 2020.

10. Pope Leo XIII. "Rerum Novarum: Encyclical of Pope Leo
XIII on Capital and Labor." Holy See, 14 May 1891, www
.vatican.va/content/leo-xiii/en/encyclicals/documents/hf_l
-xiii_enc_15051891_rerum-novarum.html.

11. Rubio, Marco. "What Economics Is For." *First Things*, 26
Aug. 2019, www.firstthings.com/web-exclusives/2019/08/what
-economics-is-for.

12. Pfeffer, Jeffrey. *Dying for a Paycheck: How Modern Management
Harms Employee Health and Company Performance—and What
We Can Do About It*. New York: Harper Business, 2018.

13. Walsh, Dylan. "The Workplace Is Killing People and Nobody
Cares." *Insights by Stanford Business*, 15 Mar. 2018, www.gsb
.stanford.edu/insights/workplace-killing-people-nobody-cares.

14. "France Télécom Suicides: Three Former Bosses Jailed." BBC
News, 20 Dec. 2019, www.bbc.com/news/world-europe-50865211.

15. Nossiter, Adam. "3 French Executives Convicted in Suicides of 35 Workers." *New York Times*, 20 Dec. 2019, www.nytimes .com/2019/12/20/world/europe/france-telecom-suicides.html.

Chapter 5: The Heartlessness of the Matter

1. Baylor University. "Supervisors, Coworkers Tolerate Unethical Behavior When Production Is Good, Study Finds." *Science-Daily*. 5 Apr. 2016, www.sciencedaily.com/releases/2016/04 /160405095015.htm.

2. Christoff, Kalina. "Dehumanization in Organizational Settings: Some Scientific and Ethical Considerations." *Frontiers in Human Neuroscience*, 24 Sep. 2014, doi:10.3389/fnhum.2014.00748.

3. Choi, BongKyoo. "Job Strain, Long Work Hours, and Suicidal Ideation in US Workers: A Longitudinal Study." *International Archives of Occupational and Environmental Health*, vol. 91, no. 7, 2018, pp. 865–875, doi:10.1007/s00420-018-1330-7.

4. Hempstead, Katherine A., and Julie A. Phillips. "Rising Suicide Among Adults Aged 40–64 Years: The Role of Job and Financial Circumstances." *American Journal of Preventive Medicine* vol. 48, no. 5, 2015, pp. 491–500, doi:10.1016/j.amepre .2014.11.006.

5. Walsh, Dylan. "The Workplace Is Killing People and Nobody Cares." *Insights by Stanford Business*, 15 Mar. 2018, www.gsb .stanford.edu/insights/workplace-killing-people-nobody-cares.

6. Cross, Rob, Reb Rebele, and Adam Grant. "Collaborative Overload." *Harvard Business Review*, Jan.–Feb. 2016, hbr.org /2016/01/collaborative-overload.

7. Chui, Michael, James Manyika, and Mehdi Miremadi. "Where Machines Could Replace Humans—and Where They Can't (Yet)." *McKinsey Quarterly*, July 2016, www.mckinsey .com/business-functions/mckinsey-digital/our-insights /where-machines-could-replace-humans-and-where-they -cant-yet.

8. Selyukh, Alina. "Walmart Is Eliminating Greeters. Workers with Disabilities Feel Targeted." NPR, 25 Feb. 2019, www .npr.org/2019/02/25/696718872/walmart-is-eliminating -greeters-workers-with-disabilities-feel-targeted.

9. Selyukh, Alina. "Walmart Is Eliminating Greeters. Workers with Disabilities Feel Targeted." NPR, 25 Feb. 2019, www .npr.org/2019/02/25/696718872/walmart-is-eliminating -greeters-workers-with-disabilities-feel-targeted.

10. Nassauer, Sarah. "Walmart Store Managers Make $175,000 a Year on Average." *Wall Street Journal*, 8 May 2019, www.wsj .com/articles/walmart-store-managers-make-175-000-a-year -11557339360.

11. Meyersohn, Nathaniel. "Walmart CEO Doug McMillon's Total Pay Was Nearly $24 Million Last Year." CNN, 24 Apr. 2019, www.cnn.com/2019/04/23/business/walmart-ceo-doug -mcmillon-pay-retail/index.html.

12. Walmart. "Walmart U.S. Q4 Comp Sales(1) Grew 4.2% and Walmart U.S. ECommerce Sales Grew 43%, Q4 2019 GAAP EPS of $1.27." corporate.walmart.com/newsroom/2019/02/19 /walmart-u-s-q4-comp-sales1-grew-4-2-and-walmart-u-s -ecommerce-sales-grew-43-q4-2019-gaap-eps-of-1-27.

Chapter 6: Unsafety in Numbers

1. Caro, Robert. *The Power Broker*. New York: Knopf, 1974.

2. Caro, Robert. *The Power Broker*. New York: Knopf, 1974.

3. Schwartz, Nelson D., and Michael Corkery. "When Sears Flourished, So Did Workers. At Amazon, It's More Complicated." *New York Times*, 23 Oct. 2018, www.nytimes.com/2018/10/23 /business/economy/amazon-workers-sears-bankruptcy-filing .html.

4. Friedman, Milton. "The Social Responsibility of Business Is to Increase Its Profits." *New York Times Magazine*, 13 Sept. 1970, http://umich.edu/~thecore/doc/Friedman.pdf.

5. Friedman, Milton. "The Social Responsibility of Business Is to Increase Its Profits." *New York Times Magazine*, 13 Sept. 1970, http://umich.edu/~thecore/doc/Friedman.pdf.

6. Jensen, Michael C., and Kevin J. Murphy. "CEO Incentives— It's Not How Much You Pay, But How." *Harvard Business Review*, May–June 1990, hbr.org/1990/05/ceo-incentives-its -not-how-much-you-pay-but-how.

7. Mishel, Lawrence, and Julia Wolfe. "CEO Compensation Has Grown 940% Since 1978." Economic Policy Institute, 14 Aug. 2019, www.epi.org/publication/ceo-compensation-2018/.

8. Eavis, Peter, and Anupreeta Das. "Rare Stock Tweak During Pandemic Adds Millions to a C.E.O.'s Potential Payout." *New York Times*, 4 June 2020, www.nytimes.com/2020/06/04 /business/raytheon-ceo-stock.html.

9. Enrich, David, and Rachel Abrams. "McDonald's Sues Former C.E.O., Accusing Him of Lying and Fraud." *New York Times*, 10 Aug. 2020, www.nytimes.com/2020/08/10/business /mcdonalds-ceo-steve-easterbrook.html.

10. Holson, Laura M. "Ruling Upholds Disney's Payment in Firing of Ovitz." *New York Times*, 10 Aug. 2005, www.nytimes .com/2005/08/10/business/media/ruling-upholds-disneys -payment-in-firing-of-ovitz.html.

11. Rawls, John. *A Theory of Justice*. Cambridge, MA: Harvard University Press, 1971.

12. Christoff, Kalina. "Dehumanization in Organizational Settings: Some Scientific and Ethical Considerations." *Frontiers in Human Neuroscience*, 24 Sep. 2014, doi:10.3389/fnhum.2014.00748.

13. Christoff, Kalina. "Dehumanization in Organizational Settings: Some Scientific and Ethical Considerations." *Frontiers in Human Neuroscience*, 24 Sep. 2014, doi:10.3389/fnhum.2014.00748.

14. Terdiman, Daniel. "Welcome to 'the Matrix': At FedEx's Sorting Hub, 1 Night, 1.5M Packages." CNET, 12 July 2014, www.cnet .com/news/at-fedex-sorting-packages-1-5-million-at-a-time/.

15. Risher, Wayne. "FedEx Investing $1 Billion to Expand Its Memphis Hub, Improve Network." *USA Today*, 14 Mar. 2018,

www.usatoday.com/story/money/nation-now/2018/03/14
/fedex-investing-1-billion-expand-its-memphis-hub-improve
-network/424574002/.

16. Good Jobs First. "FedEx: Violation Tracker." violationtracker
.goodjobsfirst.org/parent/fedex.

17. Risher, Wayne. "Tennessee Cites FedEx for Fatal Accident,
Proposes $4,000 Fine." *Transport Topics*, 18 May 2016, www
.ttnews.com/articles/tennessee-cites-fedex-fatal-accident
-proposes-4000-fine.

18. DiCasimirro, Gemma, and Kurt Chirbas. "FedEx Worker
Dies Unloading Plane at Memphis International Airport."
NBC News, 24 Nov. 2017, www.nbcnews.com/news/us-news
/fedex-worker-dies-unloading-plane-memphis-international
-airport-n823741.

19. "Family of FedEx Employee Killed in Accident Sues Equipment
Makers." WMC5 *Action News*, 14 Nov. 2018, www.wmcaction
news5.com/2018/11/14/family-fedex-employee-killed-accident
-sues-equipment-makers/.

20. "FedEx to Pay Millions in Retaliation Case." NBC Los Angeles, 7
Nov. 2018, www.nbclosangeles.com/local/fedex-to-pay-millions
-in-retaliation-case/144180/.

21. Sherman, Erik. "FedEx Latest Company Slammed Over
'Independent' Employees." *Forbes*, 3 Sept. 2014, www.forbes
.com/sites/eriksherman/2014/09/03/fedex-latest-company
-slammed-over-independent-employees.

22. DePillis, Lydia. "How FedEx Is Trying to Save the Business
Model That Saved It Millions." *Washington Post*, 23 Oct. 2014,
www.washingtonpost.com/news/storyline/wp/2014/10/23
/how-fedex-is-trying-to-save-the-business-model-that
-saved-it-millions/.

23. Lamansky, Katrina. "FedEx Worker Found Dead Outside East
Moline Delivery Hub." WQAD, 31 Jan. 2019, www.wqad.com
/article/news/local/drone/8-in-the-air/body-of-fedex-worker
-found-outside-east-moline-delivery-hub/526-fbb51b6e-299a
-4a5d-80e4-4c42e9c0bb3b.

24. Seville, Lisa Riordan, et al. "In the Hot Seat: UPS Delivery Drivers at Risk of Heat-Related Illnesses." NBC News, 18 July 2019, www.nbcnews.com/business/economy/hot-seat-ups -delivery-drivers-are-risk-heat-stroke-kidney-n1031321.

25. H-E-B. "H-E-B Deploys Mobile Kitchen to SE Texas, Sends Aid to Louisiana Food Banks." H-E-B Newsroom, 28 Aug. 2020, newsroom.heb.com/h-e-b-deploys-mobile-kitchen-to-se -texas-sends-aid-to-louisiana-food-banks/.

Chapter 7: Home Ice Is Where the Heart Is

1. Magids, Scott, Alan Zorfas, and Daniel Leemon. "The New Science of Customer Emotions." *Harvard Business Review*, Nov. 2015, hbr.org/2015/11/the-new-science-of-customer-emotions.

2. Mohammed, Rafi. "After a Blizzard, What's a Fair Price for a Shovel?" *Harvard Business Review*, 11 Feb. 2013, hbr .org/2013/02/after-a-blizzard-whats-a-fair.

3. Thaler, Richard H. "From Cashews to Nudges: The Evolution of Behavioral Economics." *American Economic Review*, vol. 108, no. 6, June 2018, pp. 1265–1287, doi:10.1257/aer.108.6.1265.

4. AP. "A Tale of Two Arenas: Islanders Fans Prefer the Coliseum." *USA Today*, 30 Jan. 2019, www.usatoday.com /story/sports/nhl/2019/01/30/a-tale-of-two-arenas-islanders -fans-prefer-the-coliseum/38976503/.

5. Albanese, Laura. "Gary Bettman Still Noncommittal on Islanders Games at Coliseum." *Newsday*, 25 Jan. 2020, www.newsday .com/sports/hockey/islanders/islanders-nhl-gary-bettman-1 .40977288.

6. Compton, Brian. "Tavares Signs Seven-Year Contract with Maple Leafs." NHL, 1 July 2018, www.nhl.com/news/john-tavares -signs-seven-year-deal-with-toronto-maple-leafs/c-299370932.

7. Governor Andrew M. Cuomo. "Governor Cuomo Announces New York Islanders to Return to Long Island Next Season— Three Years Ahead of Schedule." New York State, 29 Jan. 2018, www.governor.ny.gov/news/governor-cuomo-announces-new

-york-islanders-return-long-island-next-season-three-years -ahead.

8. Staple, Arthur. "Islanders' Return to Nassau Coliseum Creates Playoff Atmosphere." *Newsday*, 18 Sept. 2017, www.newsday .com/sports/hockey/islanders/islanders-return-to-nassau -coliseum-creates-playoff-atmosphere-1.14203031.

9. Kreda, Allan. "Islanders Return to Nassau Coliseum, Thrilling Fans and Players Alike." *New York Times*, 1 Dec. 2018, www .nytimes.com/2018/12/01/sports/islanders-nassau-coliseum .html.

10. Gross, Andrew. "Ex-Islander Calvin de Haan Says Hurricanes Benefited from Avoiding Nassau Coliseum." *Newsday*, 2 May 2019, www.newsday.com/sports/hockey/islanders/nassau -coliseum-hurricanes-calvin-de-haan-1.30555112.

Chapter 8: The New MBA: Master of Business Amelioration

1. "One Million Species to Go Extinct 'Within Decades.'" Al Jazeera, 6 May 2019, www.aljazeera.com/news/2019/05/06 /one-million-species-to-go-extinct-within-decades/.

2. "American Business Schools Are Reinventing the MBA." *The Economist*, 2 Nov. 2019, www.economist.com/business /2019/11/02/american-business-schools-are-reinventing -the-mba.

3. Jenkin, Matthew. "Millennials Want to Work for Employers Committed to Values and Ethics." *The Guardian*, 5 May 2015, www.theguardian.com/sustainable-business/2015/may/05 /millennials-employment-employers-values-ethics-jobs.

4. Chamberlain, Andrew, and Daniel Zhao. "The Key to Happy Customers? Happy Employees." *Harvard Business Review*, 19 Aug.2019,hbr.org/2019/08/the-key-to-happy-customers-happy -employees.

5. Oliver, Laura. "Millennials Want to Work for Employers with a Purpose Beyond Profit." *AAT Comment*, 18 July 2017,

www.aatcomment.org.uk/career/millennials-want-to-work
-for-employers-with-a-purpose-beyond-profit/.

6. Dvorak, Nate, and Bailey Nelson. "Few Employees Believe in Their Company's Values." Gallup, 13 Sept. 2016, news .gallup.com/businessjournal/195491/few-employees-believe -company-values.aspx.

7. Graham, John R., et al. "Corporate Culture: Evidence from the Field." National Bureau of Economic Research, Mar. 2017, doi:10.3386/w23255.

8. Durinski, Tiffany. "2020 Engagement & Retention Report." Achievers, 30 Jan. 2020, www.achievers.com/resources/white -papers/2020-engagement-retention-report.

9. Twenge, Jean M., et al. "Generational Differences in Work Values: Leisure and Extrinsic Values Increasing, Social and Intrinsic Values Decreasing." *Journal of Management*, vol. 36, no. 5, 2010, pp. 1117–1142, doi:10.1177/0149206309352246; Goler, Lori, et al. "The 3 Things Employees Really Want: Career, Community, Cause." *Harvard Business Review*, 20 Feb. 2018, hbr.org/2018/02/people-want-3-things-from-work-but-most -companies-are-built-around-only-one.

10. *The 2017 Deloitte Millennial Survey*. New York: Deloitte, 2017, www2.deloitte.com/content/dam/Deloitte/global/Documents /About-Deloitte/gx-deloitte-millennial-survey-2017-executive -summary.pdf.

11. Boulding, William. Personal interview. 11 Nov. 2019.

12. University of Chicago. "UChicago's 531st Convocation Ceremony." YouTube, 9 June 2018, www.youtube.com/watch?v=ZSUkm 7K0jHI.

13. Marsh, James, dir. *Man on Wire*. London: BBC Storyville, 2008.

14. Viney, Donald Wayne. "William James on Free Will: The French Connection." *History of Philosophy Quarterly*, vol. 14, no. 1, 1997, pp. 29–52, www.jstor.org/stable/27744729.

15. James, William. *The Will to Believe*. New York: Dover, 1960.

Chapter 9: The Will to Believe

1. Weingarten, Carol P., and Timothy J. Strauman. "Neuroimaging for Psychotherapy Research: Current Trends." *Psychotherapy Research*, vol. 25, no. 2, 2015, pp. 185–213, doi:10.1080/105033 07.2014.883088.

2. Beauregard, Mario. "Functional Neuroimaging Studies of the Effects of Psychotherapy." *Dialogues in Clinical Neuroscience*, vol. 16, no. 1, 2014, pp. 75–81, www.ncbi.nlm.nih.gov/pmc /articles/PMC3984893/.

3. Footnote. "About." 2020, footnote.co/about/.

4. Kann, Drew, et al. "The Most Effective Ways to Curb Climate Change Might Surprise You." CNN, 19 Apr. 2019, edition.cnn.com /interactive/2019/04/specials/climate-change-solutions-quiz/.

5. Yglesias, Matthew. "The Emerging 737 Max Scandal, Explained." *Vox*, 29 Mar. 2019, www.vox.com/business-and-finance/2019/3 /29/18281270/737-max-faa-scandal-explained.

6. Gelles, David. "Costs for Boeing Start to Pile Up as 737 Max Remains Grounded." *New York Times*, 12 Apr. 2019, www .nytimes.com/2019/04/12/business/boeing-planes-economy .html.

7. Domonoske, Camila. "Boeing Brings 100 Years of History to Its Fight to Restore Its Reputation." NPR, 20 Mar. 2019, www.npr.org/2019/03/20/705068061/boeing-brings-100 -years-of-history-to-its-fight-to-restore-its-reputation.

8. Gregg, Aaron, et al. "At Tense Meeting with Boeing Executives, Pilots Fumed About Being Left in Dark on Plane Software." *Washington Post*, 14 Mar. 2019, www.washingtonpost.com /business/economy/new-software-in-boeing-737-max-planes -under-scrutiny-after-second-crash/2019/03/13/06716fda -45c7-11e9-90f0-0ccfeec87a61_story.html.

9. Cameron, Doug, and Benjamin Katz. "Boeing Orders Fall to 16-Year Low." *Wall Street Journal*, 14 Jan. 2020, www.wsj.com /articles/boeing-orders-fall-to-16-year-low-11579018235.

10. Josephs, Leslie. "Boeing's Fired CEO Muilenburg Walks Away with More Than $60 Million." CNBC, 10 Jan. 2020, www.cnbc.com/2020/01/10/ex-boeing-ceo-dennis-muilenburg-will-not-get-severance-payment-in-departure.html.

11. Robinson, Peter, and Julie Johnson. "Boeing's Push to Make Training Profitable May Have Left 737 Max Pilots Unprepared." *Bloomberg*, 29 Dec. 2019, www.bloomberg.com/news/articles/2019-12-20/boeing-s-profit-push-may-have-left-737-max-pilots-unprepared.

12. Premack, Rachel. "Here's Why FedEx Ditched Amazon and Is Throwing Itself into Powering Walmart's E-Commerce Aspirations." *Business Insider*, 5 Sept. 2019, www.businessinsider.com/fedex-ditched-amazon-walmart-ecommerce-2019-9.

13. Ziobro, Paul. "UPS Bets on Amazon, for Now." *Wall Street Journal*, 11 Aug. 2019, www.wsj.com/articles/ups-bets-on-amazon-for-now-11565521201.

Chapter 10: Project Socrates

1. Shakespeare, William. *Hamlet*. Edited by Robert S. Miola. New York: W. W. Norton, 2019.

2. Romeo, Rachel R., et al. "Beyond the 30-Million-Word Gap: Children's Conversational Exposure Is Associated with Language-Related Brain Function." *Psychological Science*, vol. 29, no. 5, May 2018, pp. 700–710, doi:10.1177/0956797617742725.

3. Nasios, Grigorios, Efthymios Dardiotis, and Lambros Messinis. "From Broca and Wernicke to the Neuromodulation Era: Insights of Brain Language Networks for Neurorehabilitation." *Behavioural Neurology*, vol. 2019, 22 Jul. 2019, doi:10.1155/2019/9894571.

4. Herwig, Uwe, et al. "Neural Activity Associated with Self-Reflection." *BMC Neuroscience*, vol. 13, no. 52, 2012, doi:10.1186/1471-2202-13-52.

Index

abulia, 78–81, 84, 155, 177, 223
Accenture, 12
accountability, 54
active inquiry, 7–10
  behavioral economics and, 156
  benefits of, 208–212
  cognitive behavioral therapy
    (CBT) compared to, 191
  consulting firm vignette, 218
  core characteristics for success, 12
  COVID-19 as dilemma
    tailor-made for, 219
  as data-gathering tool, 18,
    66–67, 71
  environmental change and,
    195–196
  evidence-based thinking and, 66
  Footnote and, 194–195
  as force against
    dehumanization, 209
  humanizing conversations via, 99
  information about the mental
    states of others, 61
  as integrator of systems 1 and
    2, 213

knowing yourself, 212
lack of, 90–92
leading to divergent thinking,
  creativity, innovation, and
  growth, 67
in medical setting, 76–77
moral and ethical value of,
  208–210
morbidity and mortality
  (M&M) conferences, 71–72
neglecting to deploy, 82–83
New York Islanders and,
  163–164, 171–172
open-ended questions, 26,
  66–67, 89, 91, 122, 156, 214
placing high value on, 218
postmortem assessment, 86
in Samaritans methodology, 76
social media as antithesis of,
  90
system 2 thinking, 95, 213
talk before you leap, 81–83
Think Talk Create as practicum
  for, 8
Walmart greeters and, 122

245

David Brendel, MD, PhD, is a board-certified psychiatrist and executive coach based in Boston. He received an MD from Harvard Medical School and a PhD in philosophy from the University of Chicago. His writings have appeared in the *Harvard Business Review* and he is the author of *Healing Psychiatry: Bridging the Science/Humanism Divide* (MIT Press).

Ryan Stelzer is a management consultant based in Boston. He served in the Obama White House as a presidential management fellow, where he and his team were responsible for optimizing performance across federal agencies. He received his master's degree from the University of Chicago. He delivered a TEDx Talk, and his writing has appeared in the *Washington Post*.

Together they cofounded a consulting firm, Strategy of Mind, which offers talks, workshops, and other programs on the Think Talk Create methodology.

PublicAffairs is a publishing house founded in 1997. It is a tribute to the standards, values, and flair of three persons who have served as mentors to countless reporters, writers, editors, and book people of all kinds, including me.

I. F. STONE, proprietor of *I. F. Stone's Weekly*, combined a commitment to the First Amendment with entrepreneurial zeal and reporting skill and became one of the great independent journalists in American history. At the age of eighty, Izzy published *The Trial of Socrates*, which was a national bestseller. He wrote the book after he taught himself ancient Greek.

BENJAMIN C. BRADLEE was for nearly thirty years the charismatic editorial leader of *The Washington Post*. It was Ben who gave the *Post* the range and courage to pursue such historic issues as Watergate. He supported his reporters with a tenacity that made them fearless and it is no accident that so many became authors of influential, best-selling books.

ROBERT L. BERNSTEIN, the chief executive of Random House for more than a quarter century, guided one of the nation's premier publishing houses. Bob was personally responsible for many books of political dissent and argument that challenged tyranny around the globe. He is also the founder and longtime chair of Human Rights Watch, one of the most respected human rights organizations in the world.

·   ·   ·

For fifty years, the banner of Public Affairs Press was carried by its owner Morris B. Schnapper, who published Gandhi, Nasser, Toynbee, Truman, and about 1,500 other authors. In 1983, Schnapper was described by *The Washington Post* as "a redoubtable gadfly." His legacy will endure in the books to come.

Peter Osnos, *Founder*